AMBITION

THE MISSING ATTRIBUTE IN YOUR EMPLOYEES

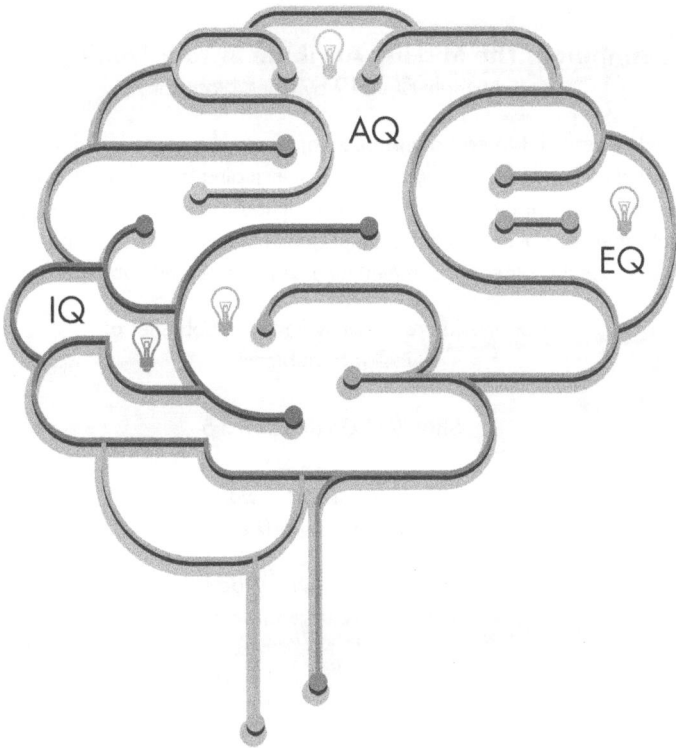

AQ

EQ

IQ

CHERYL JOHNSON

CRESTINGWAVE
PUBLISHING

Ambition: The Missing Attribute in Your Employees
Copyright © 2019 by Cheryl Johnson

ISBN: 978-0-9889048-3-5

Edited by Jyssica Schwartz
www.jyssicaschwartz.com

Illustration by Asher Wood
www.woodsquaredart.com

This book is dedicated to all those who see a need for change in the learning culture of the workplace. May you be encouraged in the struggle, find ways to innovate, and lead your organization to progress with an ever-improving process.

–

C. Johnson
Summer 2019

TABLE OF CONTENTS

INTRODUCTION

My name is Cheryl Johnson. As a performance solutions specialist, I have spent my professional life developing solutions to enable people to perform at their best.

My primary area of focus has been in the workplace, but my passion began as a mother of four children. As parents, we often focus on making sure our children get the best "education" by selecting premier preschools, making sure our kids get all A's, and helping them shoot for the best colleges. Instead of focusing solely on traditional education, I spent much time reading to my kids, exploring nature with them, and letting them design and develop their own plays. The goal was to stimulate curiosity, to instill in them a deep love of learning so the rest would fall in place. Success in school and life would be a byproduct of their encouraged interest in continual learning.

Another element I've found to be critical to success is to learn how to deal with failure in a positive and productive way. Failure is what propels us to learn and achieve more. You cannot succeed if a failure destroys you. Unfortunately, too many young people are entering the workforce unable to deal with failure. They struggle to cope with challenges in a positive way that will benefit not only them, but also their employers. Failure is to learning as water is to plants. It is crucial to enable plants to not only survive but thrive. Failure is not a stigma or an option to avoid, but rather, it is a requirement for the type of deep learning needed to bring about real change in behavior.

I wrote **Ambition: The Missing Attribute in Your Employees** because I've seen a need to change the way we approach learning, and in particular, how information is delivered. Since the advent of online learning at the turn of the century, many new delivery methods have been introduced. The change is already happening and continues to this day, but it is not yet fully understood or realized. For the last decade, new methods for delivery have been introduced, with some achieving a higher rate of adoption than others.

- Initially, the type of online learning introduced in the early part of the century caught on rapidly, but ultimately it was limited, as it was primarily online reading with some pretty pictures.

- Then, **interactive games and simulations** entered the field. The cost of entry was high, as well as the cost and time needed to maintain and update the games and simulations, so it was not widely adopted.

- **Knowledge management** was the next trend. It was not difficult to adopt, as it mostly consisted of reusing tools already in use for a long time, but now being implemented from different platforms, such as job aids, white papers, and others. These are typical forms of knowledge management.

- Then **microlearning** emerged. Due to the low cost of entry and the ease of keeping it updated, short microbursts of information were created and distributed. The only issue with microlearning was: it wasn't the solution for every challenge. Information doesn't always yield transformation, and with this learning method, change didn't necessarily happen through engaging new information once for a short period. To be effective, microlearning needs to be one facet of a more significant learning program.

Observing the recent history and evolution of online learning, it seems clear learning needs to happen everywhere, all the time, and come in many formats for individuals and businesses to remain viable in the years to come. A varied approach to staying ahead of the curve keeps you relevant, and your skills sharp. Learning to differentiate trends or fads from actual change provides valuable insight in preparing organizations for the future.

Many industries are currently in the throes of significant disruption, and companies have had various strategies for handling it. There were plenty of people who anticipated it and prepared themselves and their organizations. These people and their companies are not only still in business today, but they're thriving. Others saw disruption coming and thought waiting until the dust settled would help avoid any risky ventures which might tank their business. Others still don't see it happening and are locked into a state of "getting the job done"—unaware the world is changing rapidly.

Where are you? Are you prepared and moving forward with vigor? Are you still a bit cautious, waiting to see if the latest trend will pass? Or are you so busy doing your day-to-day tasks you don't have time to acquire new knowledge, learn new skills, or see the rapidly changing landscape in the world of learning?

> *"You can teach a student a lesson for a day, but if you can teach him to learn by creating curiosity, he will continue the learning process as long as he lives."*
> *- Clay P. Bedford*

For decades, the role of the instructional designer has been to create traditional classroom learning and, since the beginning of the century, online learning. The core way we've done this has changed very little.

We've tweaked it to make it more engaging rather than knowledge-based. We've talked for the last 20 years about how to make it performance-based and measurable—but this talk was only at conferences or around the water cooler. Only recently has talk become a reality!

We are finally here.

We're still in the midst of disruption and change. I have since switched my focus from helping organizations to helping individuals who genuinely want to learn more about the future of learning. I have gained my knowledge in the furnace of affliction and the real world of the workplace. I have owned and operated my own business for 30+ years. I have hired many young people, some of whom have gone on to work for companies in Silicon Valley along with Disney and major defense contractors as scientists, graphic artists, and world-class programmers. I've also worked with young people who have different kinds of ambitions, whether that's being stay-at-home moms, building their own businesses, or growing and learning as people, not within the context of corporate jobs.

I have also worked with some individuals who did not quite grasp what it meant to be a world-class employee when they started with me, but by the end of our time together, they'd increased their skill base and were able to move forward with newfound skills.

I am currently working for a major university with a group of students hired under a grant to teach students business analytical skills. After two failed mentors, I was hired to help them cultivate a culture of learning, support, accountability, and teamwork while developing business analytical skills. It has been both a challenge and a joy.

My company, Read, Write, & Learn Technology, LLC (RWL Tech, LLC), has been in the business of helping organizations take ordinary employees and make them extraordinary. We have used learning as a tool to make that happen for organizations all over the country.

With this book, I am hoping to share some of my journey and impart many of the lessons I have learned while directly mentoring others and building mentorship programs. The goal, in the end, is, and always will be, to help people find value in learning because learning is a crucial component to driving ambition.

I am here to share in your journey and collaborate with you as you navigate the turbulent waters ahead. I will share the vast amount of knowledge and experience I have acquired and get down in the trenches to help you problem-solve and propose solutions. I will walk this path with you.

CHAPTER 1

IQ, EQ, AND AMBITION QUOTIENT™

Learning hinges on three things: IQ, EQ, and AQ. Independently, each of these qualities provides unique value. Together, they are a formula for success.

$$IQ + EQ + AQ = SUCCESS$$

1.1 What is the Intelligence Quotient?

Your intelligence quotient (IQ) is a numerical score derived from standardized tests that assess your intelligence. The term comes from Germany and was coined by William Stern, a psychologist writing in the early 1900s. The score involves both a person's "mental age score" and his/her performance on the test. The results are multiplied by 100 to obtain the IQ score. Roughly two-thirds of the population scores between 85 and 115. Less than 3 percent of the population scores above 130, and approximately the same percentage scores below 70. In other words, an IQ test measures a person's aptitude (his/her intelligence).

For years, schools and employers subtly (and sometimes not so subtly) implied that having a high IQ was a positive indicator of future success. However, not all types of intelligence can be measured by one standardized test.

1.2 What is the Emotional Intelligence Quotient?

Emotional intelligence (EQ) is a term created by researchers Peter Salovey and John Mayer. Author and Rutgers psychologist Daniel Goleman subsequently brought it to a broader audience in his 1996 book titled *Working with Emotional Intelligence*. Your EQ is your ability not only to understand and manage your own emotions, but also to recognize, understand, and even *influence* emotions in other people.

EQ is divided into five categories:

1. Self-awareness
2. Self-regulation
3. Motivation
4. Empathy
5. Social skills

Self-awareness is how "clued in" you are to your own emotions and how they affect other people. It involves a recognition of your inner self; including your strengths and abilities.

Self-regulation, by contrast, is your ability to contain and control your emotions, where appropriate. A leader who possesses good self-regulation can stay calm, treat others with respect, avoid emotional outbursts, and work well under pressure.

Motivation is your drive to achieve your goals and the desire to hold your work to high standards.

Empathy is the ability to understand how others feel and how your words and actions affect the emotions of those with whom you interact.

Social skills encompass how you interact with other people, manage your communications with them, and resolve or preempt conflict.

EQ, in other words, explains the role emotions play in our lives. Goleman argued EQ, more so than IQ, was an indicator of future success and cited research from Harvard to back it up. More recent Harvard Business Review writings support this case.

1.3 What is the Ambition Quotient™ (AQ)?

Even if we all agree having a reasonable IQ and developing an active EQ can help facilitate our success, we are overlooking something critical to success. The missing piece is the Ambition Quotient™, also called AQ. AQ is the driver, the determination and motivation inspiring you to get out of bed every day and achieve your dreams.

Smart people who can manage their emotions will find a level of success and may have a tremendous impact on the personal and professional development of others, but the one factor that will take them individually to the top is developing a strong AQ.

Think of AQ as cream rising to the top of the IQ-EQ-AQ equation. The cream is the sweetest part of the milk. While the milk itself is valuable and delicious, the cream takes value and delectability to a new level. This is what it means to embrace AQ. With a reasonable IQ and an active EQ, you will succeed. Developing a powerful AQ, however, will propel you to achieve excellence in all you do.

In short, your AQ is not something to be measured by standardized tests like your IQ. It can be reflected to some degree in your EQ. Your AQ lies in your ability to take your intelligence and emotional stability and translate them to a higher degree of success at home and at work, using your ambition.

We hear a lot about grit, persistence, and drive. AQ is all of those and more. It is the total of your IQ, EQ, grit, tenacity, and drive. The best part about AQ is: it does not happen at birth or genetically. It is *learned.* Learning is the key to growing and cultivating your AQ and being able to combine it with your IQ and EQ to make you and your employees highly successful.

$$IQ + EQ + AQ = SUCCESS$$

CHAPTER 2

WHAT DO EMPLOYERS AND EMPLOYEES WANT FROM THE WORKPLACE?

Let's talk about what employers want from their employees. Here, we will explore all of the elements of an ambitious employee and what you, as an employer, should be looking for in a new hire.

The world is in a transition state. For thousands of years, we were hunters and gatherers. From there, we moved to an agricultural model, and then the industrial revolution followed. People moved from a hunter-gatherer or farming model to jobs in factories and production facilities. Employers needed people who could follow the rules and fit into a defined structural model. Schools at the time adapted to provide such a model and endeavored to prepare students for work in those environments.

Then we moved into the information age. Some adaptation was required for students used to a formal structured environment to fit into a workplace where people were expected to seek out additional learning and knowledge on their own, without the benefit of "experts," professors, and teaching staff.

That age is coming to an end. How will we define the new phase? What will 21st-century work look like? No one knows for sure. But one thing we know, according to the many interviews I have done with employers, is employers need problem-solvers. Most kids have little to no experience solving real-world problems; they are not taught problem-solving and critical thinking in school.

According to Arianna Huffington of the *Huffington Post*, in the U.S., we do not need employees; as she sees it, the traditional job is dead. So what is Huffington looking for? She asked a potential employee this question: "Where do you see yourself in five years?"

The potential employee answered, "I don't think anyone knows what news or online journalism is going to be like in five years. I know I want to be a part of the conversation of helping create whatever it becomes."

She got the job.

Huffington wanted someone who had the wisdom to know she could not picture the industry in five years. Fine. But she also knew that what she needed in an employee transcended the boundaries of time and change. Knowledge and skills still work in today's world, but wisdom and ambition are timeless.

When you, as an employer, scan résumés for potential employees, you're probably looking for traditional information like job progression, building new skill sets, and strengths.

"One non-intuitive thing employers want to see on a résumé is failure," said Phil Rosenberg, president of reCareered.com. "Employers want to see you've tried, failed, and learned from your failure, all on a prior employer's dime. This demonstrates innovation, willingness to take risks, [and] faster reaction and response time. It is also a learning experience, and failure teaches success."

We will be diving into failure and resilience later in this book. But for now, it is essential to understand what Rosenberg is talking about here. When looking for ambitious employees, you have to look beyond the list of jobs on a résumé and search for moments of innovation, learning, and determination.

Ambitious employees most often show these five characteristics:

- Problem-solving
- Communication
- Teamwork
- Creativity
- Resilience

2.1 What Do These 5 Characteristics Have to Do with Ambitious Employees?

Problem-solving, communication skills, teamwork, creativity, and resilience are the essential skills that characterize the next generation of employees. By developing these skills, you'll have a competitive advantage. New learning ecosystems incorporate these soft skills into existing learning programs. They don't teach them separately because these skills will not be used independently from other skills, but rather in concert.

When people are challenged and allowed to let their creative juices flow, they are far more interested in solving problems, and resilience naturally follows if they are allowed to fail forward.

Organizations can foster an environment where their teams work cohesively and are eager to tackle issues as they arise. You can "teach" teamwork, creativity, or problem-solving in a classroom, but it rarely transfers into actual behavioral change. You need to create an environment where people feel safe to share their ideas, experiment (within boundaries), fail, and try again, all while armed with vetted and proven solutions.

2.2 What Does This Look Like in the Real World?

Some years ago, I began working for a hospitality company. I was hired as a contractor by the information technology department to support its corporate university. My first six months were spent helping the company solve technology challenges involving its learning platform.

As this aspect of my job was winding down, an opportunity to engage in an Action Learning program surfaced. I could obtain my master's degree through the corporate university's program while engaged in the Action Learning program. I was excited to tackle this project. The learning department was evolving from a classroom-based learning program to a digitized, online platform. I had some experience building online learning, but in no way was I an expert.

My Action Learning project included training several technical writers in the learning department to become instructional designers. Many people believe that technical writing and instructional design are the same things, but they are not. Technical writers, when engaging in the development of learning resources, create instructions for completion of a task, like documentation or procedural manuals. Many technical writers see themselves as instructional designers, but instructional designers are the architects of learning solutions. They are not merely developers; instructional designers understand how people learn, what motivates people to learn, and what learning delivery methods will best address the needs of the audience to facilitate job transfer from the learning space to the real world. Instructional designers create the learning process; technical writers explain how to use the tools involved in the newly designed process.

2.3 Gaining Buy−In for Success

I had 18 months to earn my degree. The existing corporate university had no instructional designers, only technical writers. My project, the learning program, would transform the latter into the former.

As my journey began, I was required to write a "reflection paper" on how I'd reached this point in my career and how I felt about it. From there, I had to put together a project plan with costs, timelines, milestones, and resources. As I was new to the organization, I was not exactly sure where to get all this information. This required some digging.

During this process, I got to know many people in the organization. Getting to know new people meant exposure to what I was trying to accomplish. The people with whom I was working would form the basis for my team, and ultimately, it would be through them that I accomplished my goal. For them to make my goal a priority, though, I had to get **creative**. I had to find a way to make my project vital to them and to what they did every day.

I also needed to get buy-in from the leadership team. Otherwise, they wouldn't want to part with their valuable time. I was not a sales and marketing person, so I had some things to learn to get the team on board. This required **problem-solving and creativity skills**. Getting the team working cohesively would require me to hone my **team-building skills**. I was the subject matter expert, so my job would be to build the program—but without the team's buy-in and support, I would be much less likely to succeed. The entire process and project required tenacity and **resilience**—if someone said "no" or didn't understand something, I needed to find a better way to explain what was required and how it would benefit them.

Every three months, I had to provide the school counselor with an update on the project. It needed to include the tasks I was working on, the challenges I encountered, and the successes I had achieved. After each meeting with the counselor, I had to adjust my plan based on that conversation and feedback.

Each iteration required creativity, problem-solving, teamwork, resilience, and communication. At that point in my career, I had never taken a course on any of these topics, but I needed to learn them if the project was to be successful. This went on for 18 months. In the end, I had to produce a final report with the full outcome. The reflection part of this process was invaluable. It was one of the critical tools I relied on to devise and revise the plan and keep moving it forward.

2.4 Why Teamwork Is Worth the Effort

In addition to creativity, problem-solving, resilience, and communication, we need to work collaboratively in teams. We all understand teamwork is...*work*. It's difficult. It requires gaining buy-in. It demands problem-solving and creativity. It also requires us to contend with, cope with, and learn from failure. Given all this, why do it? Why not insist on working by ourselves, free of these burdens?

The answer, of course, is teamwork isn't *just* work. Teamwork also **works**.

We are stronger together. But, in teams, we can accomplish more than we can individually. This includes problem-solving, which is critical to overcoming obstacles. Even with a creative and resilient team in place, all of whom have bought into the project and are enthusiastic about it, you cannot achieve your goals if you cannot solve the problems (both individually and as a team) you inevitably run into when working on various projects. If you can't communicate, you can't solve problems. And if you can't come back from failure, you can't even begin to attempt these other tasks.

2.5 Learning to Collaborate and Work in Teams

Learning to collaborate and work in teams should start in childhood. But it doesn't always. As an employer, you know even those who were high achievers in an academic setting may not come to the workplace well-equipped with these five attributes.

In the days before all the formal activities parents now enroll their children in existed, children played and worked mostly in informal, non-structured environments. They learned to get along mostly by trial and error. When kids in the neighborhood got together to play, they formed their own teams, set their own rules, refereed their own disputes, and generally functioned on an independent level from their adult caregivers. They used their imagination to play house and set up social hierarchies. They used balls, dolls, and other toys as props to support their creative endeavors.

When children were required to work, they did so under the tutelage of a caregiver, most of the time. They learned through observation and by making mistakes, which required them to redo the work time and again until they got it right.

Hopefully, each time they redid the job, they took the previous knowledge and experience to improve. In most cases, this provided a good foundation for building character and what we now often refer to as "mental toughness."

In today's more structured and formal activities, and in the days of every child receiving a participation award, they are often not learning how to fail, how to learn from failure, and how to work with a team for the good of the whole. If children are not getting the opportunity to learn teamwork as they play, they need to learn it in the workplace. See "Roadblocks." (https://youtu.be/eGQRpAo_hhE)

2.6 Ambition and Learning

Employers seek teams exemplifying ambition. Employees want to be ambitious. So, how do both achieve their goals? Since ambition can be learned, learning is where we should start. Cultivating a culture of learning is key to ensuring learning happens all the time, everywhere, by everyone.

By implementing your own unique culture of learning, your employees master their jobs faster, achieve more, and are more motivated. They **become** ambitious. They develop a high AQ to complement their IQ and EQ...and as such, they are poised to excel.

Productive employee learning ecosystems are designed to engage employees in learning as they work and let them define their path to success. This active engagement in learning motivates employees to produce at higher levels.

As a company, you need to be able to package resources tailored to each employee's needs into learning programs, so resources are readily available at the time he/she needs them. This creates custom learning paths for the employee and his/her current and future job roles.

Robust learning ecosystems need to be easy to access and use. They need to be context-sensitive and use responsive technology to customize the learning experience for each individual and device. This allows the learner to "learn while doing." Customized learning ecosystems enable your employees to master the knowledge, skills, and attitudes required to keep your company competitive. Complement classroom learning with work-related resources incorporated into the employees' daily work routine, so new skills, knowledge, and attitudes become a habit. A culture of learning relies on the knowledge, skills, and views of those within it.

The primary attributes great employees need are problem-solving (critical thinking), teamwork, communication, creativity, and resilience. They also need task-specific knowledge, such as familiarity with the technology required to do the job and other job specifics. Skills, on the other hand, are generally industry related.

With the shortage of well-qualified talent becoming more and more acute, your culture of learning is now critical to your success, as it reduces employee turnover because continual learning fosters engagement, job satisfaction, and advancement. Your specific culture of learning must engage and motivate employees to feel like they are making progress in their careers.

By establishing a culture of learning, continually improving it, and measuring its effectiveness, your company will always have the knowledge, skills, and attitudes necessary to stay competitive.

As an organization, you can either keep pace by creating a culture of learning or be forced to play catch-up when your competitors outpace you with their well-educated workforce. Your culture of learning enables employees to deliver on your organization's promises to strengthen its (and their) brand. Your culture of learning will make your employees more valuable to you.

It will, again, *make them ambitious.*

2.7 What Employees Want from Their Employers

Employers have expectations of their employees, but it's important to remember employees come to each job with expectations of their own. So, what do employees want? We have heard a lot about millennials and their "demands" in the workplace. They get much flack for their high expectations and what some employers view as their inability to reciprocate.

However, employees for generations have "wanted," though maybe not "expected," flexibility in work schedules, consideration for family life, and a reasonable work-life balance. But even more important than that, they want to be considered a contributor to the overall success of an organization. They want respect for their contributions and ideas, and they want to feel valued. Also, they want to learn, because they inherently know learning will lead to being a more significant contributor, gaining more respect, and feeling valued by management.

Learning is at the core of ambition.

Even if an employer provides learning programs, learning and development (L&D) professionals are falling short of delivering what employees say they *want and* **need**—learning on the job and effective coaching. L&D professionals spend most of their time focused on building online and classroom learning, which is the least effective method for people to learn to do their job well.

CIPD is a nonprofit organization for HR and people development, whose mission is to champion better work and working lives for employees. The 2016 CIPD/Halogen Employee Outlook survey of over 2,000 employees found that over the previous 12 months, more than a quarter (27 percent) said they were dissatisfied with the opportunity to grow and develop their skills in their job. So, what do employees want?

According to the same survey, three methods of training rated most useful by employees are:

- Training from peers (95%)
- Coaching (92%)
- On-the-job learning (91%)

However, despite the popularity of coaching, just 9 percent of employees said they had received it over the last 12 months.

Employers have a responsibility to provide effective learning opportunities and experiences. Employees have a responsibility to take advantage of those opportunities and put their newfound knowledge and skills to work for the employer so both can succeed.

2.8 Five Ways Business Owners Kill New Employees' Ambition and Value from the Start

When a new employee starts working for your company, he/she usually comes in with a healthy dose of enthusiasm. Unfortunately, in most cases, enthusiasm quickly fades. He/She is no longer excited to go to work and even less enthusiastic about his/her job once he/she gets to work.

When enthusiasm wanes, profit potential per employee wanes.

Enthusiasm is a temporary state. It was never meant to have a long shelf life. So, how do we change that dynamic and keep employees excited to perform at high levels and keep the company engine purring along at optimal levels?

We must channel short-term enthusiasm and turn it into long-term **ambition**. An ambitious employee is worth 10 to 100 times more than a non-ambitious employee to your bottom line.

Here are the five ways most companies (maybe even yours) squander or kill ambition, and how you can fix it starting immediately.

1. Boring them to death before they even get started.

Problem: Onboarding programs tend to be tons of information with very little substance. Executives and leaders share the mission statement, company history, company ethics and rules, and possibly play a few "getting to know you" games. Then they turn the new staff loose to...do what? Probably nothing for the first week or two as they wait patiently for computer access, badging, parking access, filling out HR paperwork, etc. There is nothing like doing "nothing" to get people excited to work!

Solution: Get them working on meaningful projects from day one with mentors for help and support. In my *Ambitious Employee Jumpstart Process*, we structure meaningful projects new employees can engage with on day one. This helps them get to know the company, the mission, their peers, and how and where to find information—all the things they're supposed to learn in new employee orientation, but seldom do.

2. Shutting them down when they share their ideas.

Problem: New employees come to work with a fresh perspective (which you probably told them your company wanted) and ideas they want to share. What do "old-timers" do? Shut them down with statements like, "That is a nice idea, but it won't work here," or "Why don't you learn how things work here before trying to change them?"

Solution: Stimulate creativity by having employees present their ideas in a well-thought-out presentation where they have taken the time to research their thoughts and possibly interview seasoned employees to find out what has been tried and what the results of their efforts yielded.

During this time, they will learn "how things work here" and, more importantly, what has not been working. It also empowers the employees to take ownership of their ideas, see them through to fruition, and experience the successes and challenges of making new ideas work. This process also allows your employees to be creative and potentially contribute great ideas to your business. Don't just dismiss new ideas because "this is the way it's always been done." Creativity and problem-solving almost always come from looking at an old problem with a fresh perspective—foster it.

3. Labeling "failure" without defining success.

Problem: When a new employee encounters aspects of his job he does not know how to complete, is your company genuinely open to him asking questions? Is there adequate training on how to do the job in the manner the company wants it completed? How is a failure (or experimentation) viewed in your organization? You're destroying ambition by allowing your employees to fail with no avenue for remediation or learning.

Solution: Allow new employees the room to grow by using appropriate risk-taking. Make sure the employee understands the rules and, most importantly, that he/she is well-managed. Having a manager checking in and working with the new employee from the beginning opens the conversation for how to do things correctly and for the employee to learn as he/she goes. Have frequent meetings and discussions about what is expected of him/her and what constitutes his/her success within your organization.

Instead of reprimands, try corrections and discussing WHY something failed. Allow your employees to learn from the failure instead of just feeling quashed.

4. Prolonged isolation makes teamwork difficult.

Problem: Some jobs (and some employees) work well in isolation, but all positions require employees to work collaboratively with/ in teams. For new (and current) employees alone "too long," collaboration can become an issue.

Solution: Teach the employees how to be team players and teach other employees how to interact with people who are "hard to get along with." You can add team-building activities into everyday work habits by starting with fun and simple activities that build trust and enable everyone to have a voice in the process. It makes teams faster, without all the fuss of traditional team-building programs. Foster and encourage your employees to work together, ask for help, and get to know their colleagues.

5. Ignoring the rough edges instead of polishing them.

Problem: Everyone makes mistakes. Everyone struggles with some aspect of their job. How your organization handles those mishaps can either make or break an employee's ambition.

Solution: Create an environment that builds resilient employees. Don't ignore mistakes; take the opportunity to teach the employee how and why something went wrong so he/she can do better next time. In my work, I often formulate process maps to help new employees work through challenges in productive and healthy ways, which ultimately can turn little mistakes into large accomplishments.

As a business owner, increasing profit potential per employee should be your ONLY focus. Employee learning and retention is a huge part of growing it.

If you want ambitious, engaged, and motivated employees who drive your profitability, their ambition needs to be tended to and

maintained every day, like any well-oiled machine. The key to driving ambition in your employees lies in how well they learn to manage all aspects of their onboarding, tenure, and ramping down periods at your organization.

2.9 Looking for Ambition When Interviewing

How can you look for characteristics and attributes predicting ambition in potential employees during the interview process? Try searching for this information.

1. Does he/she ask questions?

    a. Look past generic questions and watch for potential employees who ask the right kinds of questions about your company, learning and growth opportunities, and how management is organized. Asking good questions shows the prospective employee has done research, is interested in your company specifically, is creative in his/her approach, and can communicate effectively.

2. Does he show progression in his previous roles?

    a. Having been promoted or given additional responsibility in previous roles shows he can solve problems and work well with others, and it shows ambition itself.

    b. If the potential employee has no previous work experience, ask where she sees herself in five years. This can give you an idea of if she is looking to move up the ladder.

3. Did he send a follow-up letter after his interview?

    a. This shows he is persistent, communicates professionally, and is interested in your company.

4. His level of interest in the job.

a. With this, you are looking for if (s)he has a clear understanding of the role and how (s)he would fulfill the duties. If not, what types of things would (s)he do to get up to speed?

b. You don't want an employee who is looking for just ANY job; you're looking for one who is specifically interested in and qualified for YOUR situation.

5. Ask him this question in the interview: "Are you smart, or do you work hard?"

a. With this, you are evaluating if the applicant values IQ or AQ. Hopefully, (s)he values both, but the answer (s)he leads with will help you understand how much value (s)he puts on ambition, which gives you more information about how (s)he thinks and how (s)he works.

CHAPTER 3

COMMUNICATION

"Seek first to understand, then to be understood."
- Stephen R. Covey

Communication is a critical tool for building and reinforcing trust. What does trust have to do with ambition? For employees to feel safe enough to take even the simplest of risks, they must trust their efforts will be appreciated, even if they fall short at times. Trust thrives on a foundation of excellent communication.

How many times have you seen an interaction which should have been simple turn into a problem because the parties involved were not communicating with one another effectively? Effective communication does not merely transmit information from party to party but includes active listening and understanding of the intentions and emotions behind the words. It's an essential building block of the ambitious workforce. Only when a team communicates effectively can they interact in meaningful ways and achieve excellent outcomes.

Effective communication is not something to be taken for granted. There are multiple stumbling blocks and opportunities for improvement. When the members of a team embrace these opportunities, they not only build trust but also position the team for success. In other words, a team whose members trust each other is a team that collaborates better and achieves more.

To work well within a team and with others, you must be able to communicate effectively. To communicate effectively means being able to exchange information while offering feedback which fosters collaboration and builds trust. You must listen actively, provide thoughtful questions, process the information provided, identify what can be improved, and act to implement those improvements.

3.1 Goal–Oriented Communication

Communication may be formal or informal. Most of the communications you have are informal. You don't plan them, and you tend to say whatever you're thinking. Formal communication, however, is goal-driven. When you communicate with someone in a formal setting, and when you use communications to build teams and encourage the development of ambitious employees, you approach your interactions with a goal in mind.

Steps to Activating Goal–Oriented Communication

- First, identify your goal.

- Second, determine with whom you will communicate to reach this goal. This allows you to develop a clear, precise, and concise message, which also considers how the audience prefers to receive communication.

- Third, determine the best means of delivering your message (email, phone call, in-person meeting, etc.).

- Fourth, determine what you are asking of your audience. What can the other party or parties do to help you achieve your goal?

Often, part of the communication involves explaining the goal or goals you all share. Those with shared goals, the ones who have buy-in, are more willing to collaborate. This collaboration is what builds trust and vice versa.

3.2 Building Rapport and Encouraging Collaboration

When you communicate effectively and explain shared goals, you create a rapport with the other person or people. In other words, you are establishing relationships with them. Business relationships—specifically, positive and collaborative ones—are critical to your success and the success of your organization. Take the time to foster these relationships.

Listed below are a few methods for building rapport:

1. **Don't neglect social interaction with your teammates.** People who believe you only talk to them when you want something will be less likely to trust you and therefore less eager to collaborate. Having positive social relationships builds trust and fosters a collaborative environment.

2. **Never forget to show your appreciation for what others do for you.** Even if it is to explain you're grateful for your interactions with them, teammates who feel valued and who believe they are appreciated are much more likely to collaborate.

3. **Avoid negative social interactions (gossip, complaining, bad-mouthing, etc.) at all costs.** These destroy trust and will kill a team member's desire to collaborate.

3.3 Communicating with Your Team, and Teaching, as a Leader

As critical as communication is among team members, it is especially important for team leaders. **Leading is teaching**, and developing ambitious employees is a byproduct of meaningful teaching.

You may be cautious of the perceived scale of this task because you may not believe yourself to be an expert on this subject. The good news is: you don't have to be.

You're reading this book because you want to learn. Perhaps you already feel as if you are a good learner, and you want to do it better. Whatever your motivation, you are not alone. We are all in this together. This is no longer about my journey or yours; it is about what we, together, can achieve. It is about how we can create ambitious employees and foster an ambitious workplace.

Many people believe that to teach, you must be an expert. This is not true. A well-prepared learner can teach, benefiting both the learner and those she is teaching. In creating a culture of learning, everyone has an opportunity to share their knowledge and expertise, no matter their current level of understanding. This empowers everyone, fosters growth and development, and creates a trusting, collaborative environment in which people feel appreciated for their contributions.

3.4 Team–Driven Communications Principles

Communication is about quality, not quantity. Trust in the workplace, and therefore the desire to collaborate, is difficult to foster, even in the best of times. The 2019 Edelman Trust Barometer explains we live in a profoundly divided world. Few of us believe "the systems" in which we live and work are operating for us.

The overwhelming majority of employees (71%) believe it is critically important for the leadership of their companies to respond to challenging times. Seventy-five percent of employees trust their employers, which sounds like a high figure until you realize this means one in four employees do not trust their employers to do what is right or to tell them the truth.

About half of employees believe businesses, in general, can be trusted, and slightly fewer believe governments are trustworthy. Only 58 percent of employees trust their employers to provide "certainty." Significantly, the *Trust Barometer* shows meeting employee expectations builds *resilient* trust. The more employers perform against employee expectations, the higher the figure goes.

To develop trust and communicate according to team-driven principles, therefore, it's essential to approach communication with your team in an authentic, earnest way that aligns with how they learn best and considers their expectations and needs.

Among the most crucial team-driven communication principles are these:

1. Be authentic.
2. Learn your employees' expectations.
3. Understand your team members' different learning styles.
4. Involve your team members to engage them as active participants.
5. Follow through.

3.5 Communicating Across Generations

The workforce is always changing. A cottage industry now exists in writing articles about how millennials are changing what we take for granted in the business world (and in many other aspects of popular culture). The average multigenerational workforce includes traditionalists (those who precede the baby boomers), baby boomers (born after World War II), Generation Xers (who run from late 30s to middle age), millennials (who are now in their 20s and 30s), and members of Generation Y, who are just now old enough to enter the workforce.

Take the time to learn how different generations tend to prefer to communicate.

- **Traditionalists or "Matures"** — Highly loyal, value stability, do as they're told, and prefer direct, concise communication.

- **Baby Boomers** — More hostile to authority and appreciate having a degree of flexibility. They prefer to be engaged directly.

- **Generation X** — Value work-life balance and tend to prefer informal communications. Keep communications brief, but not curt.

- **Millennials/Generation Y** — Extremely comfortable with modern technology and the most sensitive to issues of cultural tolerance. They prefer flexibility, are easily bored, and have little loyalty to employers, requiring them to be kept engaged and incentivized.

3.6 Communicating Across Cultures

Cultural differences can lead to distinct issues where communication is concerned.

In some cultures, it is not considered acceptable to ask questions or to clarify if you do not understand something explained to you. It makes you look less than competent. Thus, there are many times when you may describe something and ask the recipient if they understand, and they will say yes when they do not understand. As you may well imagine, this can cause significant problems on a project.

To resolve this, you can ask the person to repeat back the instructions, and it will become clear if they understood your direction. This will give you a good indication of their level of understanding. We should also approach communication across cultures with the understanding we may both forget and default to our cultural perceptions. We must make a conscious effort to be aware of expectations on both sides that are not being communicated (and thus could lead to misunderstandings).

Given that every culture is different, handling cross-cultural communication is a matter of (1) learning said culture's expectations, necessities, traits, and even demands, and (2) consistently applying your awareness of these. Such consistency is the crucial (and the most difficult) aspect.

CHAPTER 4

FAILURE AND RESILIENCE

Some say failure is the mother of experience and experience is the handmaiden of knowledge. Failure—and, more importantly, the willingness to risk failure—is how we learn.

No one learns a lesson more thoroughly than someone who has failed, has taken lessons from experience, and can take his/her knowledge forward. Fear of failure, however, stops many from trying and, therefore, from learning. The ability to withstand failure, to bounce back from it, and to try despite the risks is also known as *resilience*. It is an essential attribute in ambitious employees.

4.1 Coping with "Failure"

Back when I was completing my master's degree and working with the corporate university, I was very disappointed when it turned out the learning program I was creating was never going to launch. This was a significant blow to my motivation and enthusiasm.

First and foremost, I was disappointed, as I felt all my hard work would go to waste. Secondly, I was concerned that I would not be awarded my degree because the project had, in essence, failed. After several visits with my school counselor, I was relieved to find out the success of the project was not a criterion for my grade, and I did receive my degree.

We all fail. We are human, and we make mistakes. More important than the failure itself is how we react to and learn from failing at something. Every failure is a lesson from which we must learn. Even when something is not your fault directly, internally, it can still feel as if you have failed.

Often there are factors beyond our control influencing the success or failure of our endeavors. In my corporate learning example, the vice president of the learning department quit the same month my program was set to launch. Her replacement had no interest in this project and, honestly, no interest in anyone who worked in the department. Shortly after, I quit.

She did not share the same vision for learning I did, and she made it clear her vision would win out. The technical writers, meanwhile, had no interest in changing careers. They liked what they did and had no desire to develop new skills. Ironically, all of them left the department within two years of the change in management.

So, was my project a failure? It certainly wasn't in terms of my degree. I was evaluated, in part, on my learning journey:

- What did I learn?
- How did I learn it?
- Where would I take that learning as I continued my career?
- What knowledge, skills, and attitudes did I learn and practically apply?

The good news is: the course became the foundation for a program I developed several years later—which I was able to market and sell. Besides, I learned a lot about navigating the political landscape within an organization. These were all competencies I could never gain in a classroom setting and gave me a foundation from which to build as I continued in my own business.

It was a valuable lesson about creativity, problem-solving, resilience, failure, and the value of teamwork. If any of the required elements are lacking—or if any are removed before the task is complete and the goal attained—a "failure" results. Rather than fail, how do we leverage the lessons of experience and continue? It was another valuable learning opportunity.

My motivation could have been destroyed if not for the school counselor and a program that required reflection. Through reflection, I was able to reframe a rough situation and assess its value and move forward, having learned from it. A good coach/manager can help her employees do the same. Please permit me to share a few thoughts about this remarkable lady.

Fran Szabo was my friend, my mentor, and my school counselor. We enjoyed a shared vision for learning. She was passionate about Action Learning and an asset to the teams she supervised. She nurtured their growth and demonstrated all the qualities of a great leader; vision, empathy, and the ability to bring out the best in people. Her primary goal was always centered around enabling others to reach their full potential. I will forever be grateful for my friendship with such an inspirational person.

4.2 Failure Matters

Although on some level, we know people must learn from trial and error, we go to great lengths to help them avoid any mistakes or "failure" in their lives. We put them in classes to teach them the "right" way to do things from the very beginning. We introduce them to a process that, if they follow it, will allow them to systematically succeed without the pain of making significant mistakes which can be emotionally scarring.

I read a survey many years ago which struck a chord with me. When several very successful high school students were interviewed and asked what it took to be successful in high school, you would have expected the answer to be something along the lines of "work hard, study, participate in lots of activities," etc. However, the number one answer was: *they learned to give the teachers what they wanted.*

In other words, they regurgitated facts and answered as they were expected to instead of being allowed space for critical thinking and analysis. They were puppets, not students.

We define young people by what they do, and the activities in which they participate. There are times we allow them to make their own choices, but whether by our choice or theirs, a certain sense of identity comes from the activities they choose, and they will continue throughout their young lives to define themselves by these activities and how "good" they are at them. The message we are sending them is: failure is not an option.

Resilience Is Coping with, and Learning from, Failure to Advance

Failure is one of the catalysts to success. There was a young man who struggled to learn to read. He was very good at math and pretty good in science, but reading just was not his thing. He was later diagnosed with auditory processing deficiencies. The problem was significant. Auditory processing does not mean you cannot hear—you will typically pass regular hearing tests. It merely means you do not hear sounds *correctly*. Can you imagine learning to read if you cannot hear, understand, and process sounds correctly? If you cannot read, can you imagine what life must be like at school?

By third grade, this young man started skipping school. He did not skip school to have fun with friends or go home and play video games. His school was on the outskirts of town, and there was not much but desert around the school. There was no need for a fence around the playground, so when he would go out to play, he would wander off into the desert by himself until it was time to go home. He was a very social kid but preferred to be off alone in the desert with very little to do than in a school where he felt discouraged and defeated.

As time went on, you can imagine the path he followed. Although his parents went to great lengths to provide interventions, he still struggled. He had ups and downs from year to year, but overall, he seemed to be on a downward trajectory.

He was a great football player. He played from the time he was in the youth football league and won several awards for his success on the field. However, as football demanded more and more strategic thinking patterns at the higher levels, and he was required to study and learn plays from pieces of paper, he fell behind in that area, too. He went from being the star to getting benched in his senior year of high school.

Due to much societal pressure, he went to college and played football for a small school. He did not do well there, because the focus shifted from practicing skills on the playing field to studying intricate plays. Also, the college culture of drinking and partying contributed to deficient grades. He only survived one year in college.

So, he moved several thousand miles away. He got a job building fences. He did okay in the job, but it appeared to be a dead-end job. Thus, when his uncle offered him the opportunity to work for his company, he jumped at it. He was required to go to night school and take vocational classes. He did very well in those classes because many of them were math-related.

Once again, as the classes got more advanced and required more reading and comprehension without practical application, he struggled and dropped out. He was also struggling to learn on-the-job skills because the company's model for teaching was to "learn by observation." His supervisor was a bully with little to no patience for mistakes. Even with simple things, the boss berated the kid daily for either not trying or trying and making mistakes.

So, he quit the job and went back to building fences. He continued down that road for a few years while he built his confidence and got some success under his belt. With time, he now feels like he can work with a certain level of autonomy, can work independently, and feels good about putting in a full day's work.

Was this person headed in a positive direction? I believe he was and is. Let me explain.

4.3 We Must Celebrate Resilience

Many of the obstacles he faced and the steps he took required him to work hard—probably harder than those whose success came more easily. He had to find creative solutions to learning in school, as well as learning on the football field. At work, he struggled to read and use the manual to do his work, so when working with him, we came up with a plan to put tutorials on a mobile device to quickly find processes he could not remember on the job. Due to specific struggles he had with his boss, he would often call me in the depths of despair. I admit there were times I suggested he quit, but even in a state of depression, he refused to give up. He realized he needed help and was willing to put in extra time to learn.

Schools and companies do not celebrate this type of experience. We don't get trophies for being resilient. Alternatively, if we do, it feels like a consolation prize, not the gold medal. We berate failure and do not look kindly upon those who do not follow the tried and true path to success.

This makes perfect sense on some level, but honestly, how can one get to "success" without failure? Failures become meaningful life experiences supporting learning and future success. To leverage failure and turn experiences into success, we must develop *wisdom*.

4.4 Bridging the Gap to the Real World

So, sounds great! However, we're not talking about theory. We aren't speaking in platitudes. How do we apply these concepts to creating resilient, creative, capable, ambitious problem-solvers who are poised to excel in life?

I was born into a family of naturally successful people. They did well in school and proved themselves to be leaders in sports and music; they were a naturally talented group of people. Somewhere along the line, those natural abilities did not fall to me. Sure, I could do well in school, with effort. I did okay in sports and loved dancing and playing the piano, but I was certainly not a "natural" at any of it. I had to work hard and endure challenges to get what few accolades I achieved. For years, I felt like I was less than others because I was comparing myself to those around me instead of celebrating my achievements.

Since I had to learn to do things the hard way, I learned a lot about those five characteristics of success we talked about:

- Creativity
- Problem-Solving
- Teamwork
- Communication
- Resilience

I graduated high school when I was 17, a semester ahead of my classmates. I grew up in small-town USA and dreamed of living in a big city. My aunt lived in California, and she invited me to come and live with her, which I happily did. She had a friend who owned a dental lab, and I got a job there, which involved picking up and delivering the molds needed to fit dentures, as well as making crowns for people's teeth.

I was not good at this job. It was a simple task, but I was young and thought I knew it all, and as my fourth-grade teacher always told me, I "would rather be first than accurate." I would too often rush through the process, and the molds would have to be redone. My boss was patient with me but did not give me much help when I made mistakes. After a few months, it was clear I was not "getting it." He was kind and said business was slowing and he needed to lay me off. I knew, deep down inside—I was not making the grade.

As an employer, he did have another option if I had been more willing to learn. If his business was doing well and he needed to hire a new person, was the cost of hiring and training a new person more or less than working with me to improve my skills? What I did bring to the table was ambition, dependability, reliable customer service skills, and a drive to succeed.

Was it possible to give me more "guided practice" with an observation checklist that he completed as he checked each step of the process for accuracy? There is the possibility that with a couple more practice sessions, I would have been up to speed. You may let one person go for their inability to produce the quality of work you're looking for, but remember: the new person you hire may struggle with a similar issue.

Once I was released, and after working a few temporary jobs, I was able to secure an outstanding job working for the County of Fresno as the executive secretary to the vice president of risk management. I was only 18. I am sure I got the job because I could type fast and knew shorthand well. Typing was a skill many people had, but I was fast (just not very accurate). Shorthand was my ace in the hole. Very few people could do shorthand, and once again, I was fast. I had won an award in high school for my skill in shorthand. I was a daydreamer and would spend hours listening to people talk and either physically (or in my head) writing down what they were saying in shorthand. When I watched TV, I would write down what they were saying in shorthand.

So, I got the job. However, it was not very long before I realized I was not living up to their expectations, either.

This was in the days of the old IBM Selectric typewriter with the correction tape ribbons. We used high-quality bond paper to send out letters and, of course, every letter had to be composed and delivered in perfect condition. I could generally get the letter done with all the correct words, and typos addressed, but often there would be a slight imprint on the paper where the incorrect letter was before I fixed it.

I was determined to make myself into the best executive secretary possible. I would spend my lunch hours at the library practicing my shorthand and typing skills. I learned to read documents forward and backward to improve my proofreading skills. Most importantly, I finally learned to slow down and place value on accuracy. However, after nine months and some inside information from a coworker, I saw the writing on the wall. So, I quit. Once again, would some coaching and mentoring have helped? Rather than simply express frustration at my lack of accuracy, would some encouragement and direction have changed the situation? I am not sure. But once again, back then it was probably cheaper and easier to replace me than to help me succeed. This is not the case today.

The good news is that my next job appeared quickly. I worked there for many years, and they applauded my speed, accuracy, and ambitious nature. The speed and accuracy I attribute to the jobs where I "failed."

4.5 Is It an Employer's Job to Teach Resilience?

I hear far too often employees are not coming to the market with this type of resilience. Why is that? Let's start by examining the job market. It has been said that:

1. Young people are not adequately prepared for the jobs that exist, and

2. The competition for existing jobs is getting fierce due to declining job availability.

College and career training programs can provide the knowledge and skills needed to work in today's jobs. What is lacking are the character traits we discussed. These are not taught (valued?) in school or the workplace. Colleges and vocational training programs fail to teach even the most successful students' wisdom.

FAILURE = WISDOM

How can we teach resilience so positive outcomes result from failure? The dichotomy is that we minimize risk-taking and do all we can to prevent failure when failure is the ticket to success.

To become resilient and ambitious, we must learn from past mistakes— from past failures. Self-analysis, critical thinking, and the ability to evaluate the challenges with which you've been presented (and the problems you've solved) are all part of this process. This is how wisdom is created.

Once again, we do not learn wisdom from books, writing papers, learning math, or graduating high school or college. Many graduates have taken a path to nowhere. Even though they've obtained knowledge, they do not know how to reflect on the "what can I do better" concept that leads to better choices when faced with challenges.

We learn knowledge but fail to gain wisdom: knowledge helps us find the right answers; wisdom enables us to ask the right questions.

How do we do that?

4.6 Wisdom from Failure Is Resilience in Operation

Wisdom comes from life's most challenging experiences. Wisdom enables us to define "who" we will become, not "what" we will become. In other words, the virtue in failure can be wisdom, and wisdom is another catalyst for success. How do we enable our employees to learn from experiences and turn failures at work into meaningful experiences that equal success, rather than the failure most people are accustomed to experiencing?

All of us have failed at some point. How we react to failure determines whether we go down a path of self-destruction or one ultimately leading to a productive and meaningful career. To turn failure around, we need to teach the individual to reflect on his situation, and rather than ask "Why is this happening?" ask "What can I learn from this?"

When we take on this new attitude and get additional help and support in our efforts, we move from failure to growth. This growth leads inevitably to wisdom and success.

Many people falsely believe that knowledge is wisdom. It isn't. We live in an information age, an age in which we all carry in our pockets a device providing us with the total of all the world's knowledge and entertainment (and too many cat videos). Yet few of us are genuinely "wise." This shows that knowledge alone is not enough to create wisdom. This, in turn, means knowledge alone does not generate success.

Knowledge comes through learning facts. Someone who knows a lot about a subject, such as science or history, is considered knowledgeable. However, wisdom comes from observing, having experiences, and learning from them in a way that affects future decisions and behavior.

My time working as a secretary was significantly impacted by "failures." Not only did it teach me to be more patient and slower to improve accuracy, but I also learned the value of generating error-free work. I learned to take pride in my work, and this made a tremendous impact on my ability to do a good job for future employers. I learned my work was a reflection of me, and if I wanted employers to view me in a positive light, that positive light did not come from what I said I could do, but from what I produced.

Remember: Wisdom comes from observing, experiences, and learning from them in a way that affects future decisions and behavior.

4.7 Wisdom Also Comes from Challenges

We learn wisdom from the challenges we face. Real challenges, those that inscribe in our hearts the values that breed success, do not come in a failure-proof package. They come from the school of hard knocks where failure exists. We need to teach failure to our employees in a way that opens doors to success.

We need to help our employees define success in terms of "who" they are instead of "what" they are. Once they identify the "who," the "what" comes more quickly, and we are naturally inclined to be motivated and work hard to get there.

Wisdom is the ultimate definition of character, and it is available to anyone (regardless of learning style, disability, or background). Once we seek wisdom and learn to welcome life's more challenging experiences, all else falls into place.

WHO vs. WHAT

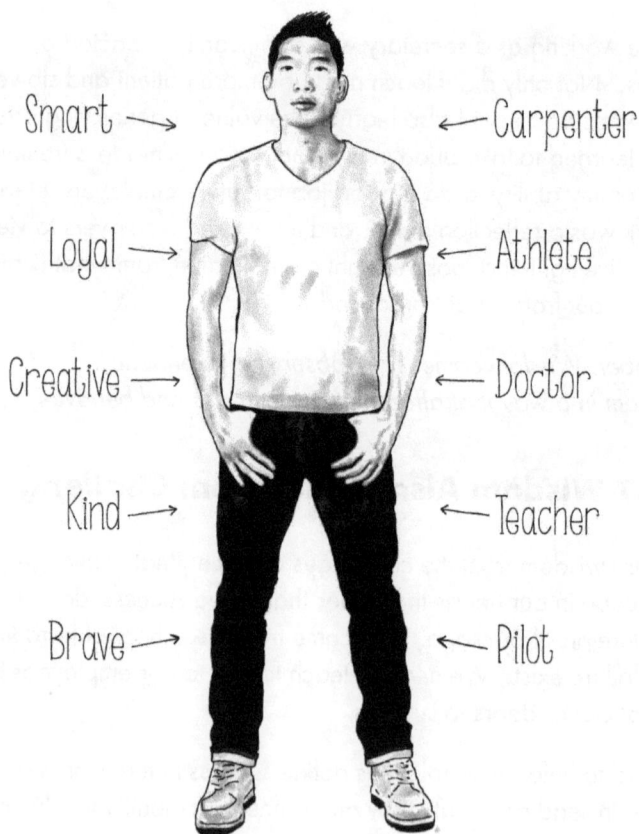

Smart →   ← Carpenter

Loyal →   ← Athlete

Creative →   ← Doctor

Kind →   ← Teacher

Brave →   ← Pilot

4.8 Coping with Adversity to Develop Ambition

What if we fail to teach people how to deal with adversity? Employees will come with a certain level of confidence and the ability to deal with adversity positively, but if your organization is one who employs many entry-level people, you are probably dealing with this issue on a different level.

If we fail to teach employees how to deal with adversity, the mine canary's warning will become a reality. The danger lies ahead as some employees continue to believe they are worthless, bad, dumb, lazy, or lacking in ambition. Also, sadly, many employers share the same view of them when they make mistakes or show a lack of initiative, which often can be attributed to a lack of understanding of the expectations of the job.

Our focus today is to teach a population that is underserved—and prepare them for life. If the cream of the crop is struggling to obtain wisdom, can you imagine what is happening to a population of youth who are not learning how to deal with the challenges life presents and making those challenges work to their advantage?

How do you teach resilience in the workplace? Resilience is not "taught" per se, but it can be coached and nurtured with empathetic managers and mentors. The coach or mentor can help the employee see where she went wrong and guide her to meaningful solutions that can encourage future attempts with newfound knowledge and wisdom.

Also, employers need to realize that mistakes are a part of growing and not punish mistakes. Mistakes should always be viewed through the lens of growth and progress. Too often we make employees feel like a failure with no path to move forward when attempts at work end up yielding negative results. Specific feedback, given with a dose of support, can go a long way toward making employees feel valued. They are more likely to share their thoughts and feelings when they do not feel like their ideas, opinions, or efforts will trigger skepticism and/ or reprimands.

Millions of young people deal with ADHD. Some of them may work for you. In school, they may be labeled worthless, bad, dumb, or lazy. Those labels stick with some of them into their adult lives. Thus, they can go from failure in school to failure at work.

If our youth who face these challenges do not learn how to deal with the unique and significant challenges they face, they will get even further behind. As they get further behind, your organization struggles, because swapping them out for a newer, better model is not the option it used to be. These are not the types of people who change the world or move your organization forward, so you must learn how to help them deal with adversity to turn them into employees who do make a positive impact.

4.9 Developing Resilience and Ambition

As a young girl, I traveled on airplanes back and forth from Alaska to Wyoming. I loved to travel, and I loved flying. When I was on the long plane rides, sometimes flight attendants would let me help them pass out playing cards and pick up trash. At 9 or 10 years old, this was a treat. As I got older, I wanted to be a flight attendant.

I don't remember my parents ever pushing or even suggesting I should be any specific thing. I don't remember them ever asking if I wanted to go to college. I knew I could do whatever I wanted and it would be up to me to make it happen. I did not have parents who agonized over every report card and berated me for bad grades (which I often would get). If I got a bad grade, they would point out I was better than that and encourage me, but I do not believe I ever heard them say anything along the lines of, "You won't get into college if you don't work on your grades."

Yet, I was an ambitious child, and I wanted to be a flight attendant. In the days before the internet, computers, and the IoT (internet of things), I had to go to the library and look up what it would take to become a flight attendant. I had to figure out which airlines were hiring, where to find applications, and how to submit them. For each airline, I had to type (on a typewriter, not a computer) each application with a cover letter, with NO mistakes. I had to address each envelope and send each one off and wait impatiently for the snail mail to come back and let me know if I'd been granted an interview.

I started this process when I was 17, because some airlines would let you work when you were 18, though most required you to be 21. Some would specify college was a plus but not a requirement. Thus, my business skills served me well, as I could submit app after app, and my waitressing skills covered the mandatory customer service requirement. Every six months, I would engage in this ritual and get the obligatory rejection letters without so much as an interview. This went on for four years.

Then one day, I got what I hoped was my big break. My brother was working in Guam, and his girlfriend was a flight attendant for Air Micronesia, a subsidiary of Continental Airlines. She said Continental was hiring. There was a higher than usual need, as the industry had just deregulated, and most airline personnel were on strike. I jumped at the opportunity. I had this ritual down pat, but Continental had never been on my list before, so I had to find its employment office.

The information I found indicated it had an office in Los Angeles, California. I submitted my application. Instead of another rejection, I got a notice saying its office had moved to Houston, Texas. Now I had the specific address and even a phone number! I wasn't going to waste any more time with letters now that I had a phone number.

I called the number and was told the recruiting team happened to be in Denver, Colorado, at the time. They said Continental was conducting interviews at a hotel by the airport. I asked which hotel, but the employee couldn't tell me. So, I looked in the phone book and found all the major hotels I could near the airport and started calling them asking for the Continental recruiting team.

I cannot recall how many hotels I called before one hotel desk clerk validated they were indeed at that hotel, and I left them a message. Surprisingly, the recruiting team called me back. The team member told me they would only be there for one more day, and if I could get there the next day, I could come to a group interview. I do not think they believed I would really do it, but I did. I jumped on a plane the next morning and attended the last group interview of the day.

Fortunately for me, the recruiting team was on its way back to the airport to return to Houston after the interview, and I was headed there too to return home. We were on the same shuttle bus! They were joking with me a bit about how they didn't think I would show up to the interview on such short notice—and pay for a plane ticket to boot. I told them my story of how I loved flying as a child and even my quasi-stewardess experience. We all had a good laugh, arrived at the airport, and went our separate ways.

The next step in the process, for those who were successful, was to have an in-person interview. In the weeks after the group interview, I waited impatiently every day for the mail to arrive, hoping for an invitation. It did not come. Then, one day, I got a telegram. I had never received a telegram in my life. When I opened it, I discovered it was an invitation to participate in flight attendant training in Houston, Texas, in two weeks. I was ecstatic! I was able to bypass the personal interview and go straight to training.

When I arrived at the training, some of the recruiters I'd met were also instructors, and the group was relatively small, so we got to know each other well. At one point, I was visiting with one of the instructors, and the subject of my recruiting experience came up. We were laughing and joking about it, and they said the primary reason they felt I would be a good fit was (a) not only were they looking for qualified candidates with customer service experience and a level-headed safety demeanor, but (b) they needed people with a high level of patience, persistence, and resilience.

The industry was in chaos due to deregulation, and they were not kidding when they said the job was more stressful than in the past. There were many cancellations, delays, re-routes, etc. After hearing my story on the shuttle, they were convinced I was the type of person who could handle that type of environment.

Now, I won't say I shined 100% of the time during those first few years, but then, to be fair, neither did anyone else. It was hard work.

However, once again, my ability to be creative, problem-solve, and demonstrate resilience in the face of adversity paid off.

I had *ambition*.

That is what employers are looking for today—and not finding in abundance. Many people have the skills necessary to complete a job, but if they don't have **ambition**, they will not find creative ways to problem-solve, work in teams, collaborate effectively, or demonstrate resilience. This is a key reason it's crucial to design an ambitious workplace by changing the way we teach so we can support the employees we have, rather than assume swapping them out for brand-new employees is a cheaper, more effective way to get results.

CHAPTER 5

LEARNING IS A NOBLE CAUSE

"I took this path because I believed strongly—and still believe—that learning is a noble cause. It is learning that has enabled human civilization and growth. It is learning that enables individuals to excel and thrive. It is learning that holds the promise of the future. If learning is so important and our task is such a noble one, don't we, as learning professionals, have an almost sacred responsibility to do our jobs well?"
- Will Thalheimer

This book, at its core, is about learning.

Specifically, it is about creating a culture of learning—*the ambition to learn*—in the workplace. Our focus is on the concept of what we call AQ. Keep in mind that this is a high-level, simplified approach to learning that will need to be modified and fleshed out in more detail for your organization and its specific requirements.

IQ + EQ + AQ = SUCCESS

In the work world, learning is viewed as a task, a boring one. Employees see it as meaningless as it serves no useful purpose to them. And truth be told, most of the learning in both school and work is boring. Employers view it as a necessary evil. It costs them money with no return on their investment. It is a cost center, not a profit generator.

But learning is the key to all of the success in the world. Learning should be a gem, every bit as valuable as diamonds. Real learning is undoubtedly as rare.

Why is learning so valuable, especially in today's environment? The world is changing and evolving so fast, and it doesn't matter whom you hire today and what skills they bring to the table—those skills will be irrelevant in five years. What are employees to do—go back to school? The cost and time commitment are far too high. What are employers to do? Hire new people with new skills? Once again, the cost and time commitment are too high.

Again, these are the five essential attributes all employers should be seeking in candidates:

- Creativity
- Problem-Solving
- Teamwork
- Communication
- Resilience

People can be taught skills, but teaching and developing that list of particular attributes is difficult, and requires more than "training." It requires *real learning*, which happens anywhere and everywhere, is easily accessible, is convenient, serves a purpose, and fills a specific need or gap.

We can blame schools, which do not encourage these types of attributes in their students, and we can blame parents for overscheduling their kids and not giving them free play to develop these skills. But we are not here to figure out how we got here; we are here to figure out how to move forward.

AQ is the desire and motivation to learn not only the skills required for the job, but also the attributes that make employees well-rounded and motivated to move the organization forward.

5.1 Real Learning

What is real learning? Real learning is that which is **acquired, absorbed,** and **applied**. Most importantly, it fills a need, a gap experienced by the learner at that moment in time. For real learning to occur, organizations must foster, nurture, and maintain a culture of learning.

5.1.1 Should Training Give You All the Answers?

The problem with learners today is that they are accustomed to being spoon-fed. When challenges arise, they do not know how to problem-solve, think creatively, and demonstrate resilience. They expect training to give them all the answers instead of opening doors to new experiences that may, at first, prove frustrating, but are rewarding when resolved. In their world, school has been there to teach them information and give them a soft landing when they could not rise above their current level of knowledge. The worst that could happen was a poor grade.

After years of navigating the school system where learning was "given" to them, they are now in a world where answers do not come easily, and people do not have time to walk them through processes step-by-step every time they ask a question. They must seek out solutions to problems they have never encountered. The solutions cannot always be recalled from memory like answers on a test.

The answer to this section's subhead is, "No, a trainer or instructor should not be simply giving people the answers." Training is where people need to be learning how to do something themselves, not just being told what to do. Let's dive into a few examples of how training at any level should work.

Example 1: A child goes to her teacher and asks for a definition of a word. The teacher does not give her a meaning. Instead, the teacher sends the girl off to find a dictionary. The girl replies, "But I don't know how to spell it; just tell me." The teacher refuses and sits with the student to sound out the word and give the girl the support and help she needs to succeed on her own.

In this example, the teacher doesn't just answer the question and move on; she gives the student the resources she needs to figure it out herself.

Example 2: A group of adult employees is attending training to learn a vital new part of their jobs. It's early, and the attendees are bored and tired. Usually, they sit there while the trainer tells them what to do and lectures. Instead, this trainer starts creating potential scenarios and asks the employees what they would do. One employee says, "You're the trainer; tell us the answer! That's why we're here." No, they are there to learn how to do it themselves and why it's essential, not just to memorize steps. The trainer continues with scenarios and has the group come up with different ways to attack the problem, explaining how and why different solutions might work or not. The employees leave with a better grasp of the new steps and written instructions to follow when they need help.

In this example, the trainer is forcing the employees to think through the problem critically and come up with potential solutions. The training is the place for employees to make mistakes and give wrong answers, so they learn why doing it the right way is important. Attendees go from bored and disinterested to involved and engaged.

Example 3: Many years ago, I started a software business with my husband. I had to attend a training session across the country in Boston in the dead of winter. Snow and delayed flights meant we got there and had to participate in the training on no sleep. We were given a manual and told to follow it step by step. I was exhausted, the computer I was using wasn't working, and it felt like a colossal waste of money. Every time something wasn't working, a tech support person had to come in and troubleshoot the issue. Each time, I watched the tech person search for and fix the problem while all of the other attendees moved ahead of me in the manual.

I was extremely frustrated during the entire training session, and when I went home, I wanted to quit. Instead, I pulled out the manuals and got to work on my own. When we took on clients, in addition to teaching my clients to use the software, I found I was able to troubleshoot and help them fix the issues they had with their computers. The other attendees of the training session were having a harder time working with their clients. Every single time something broke, they had to call tech support and try to identify the issue before being walked through how to fix it. This was before cell phones existed and long before tech support could remotely access computers to fix things. All that frustration with the hardware in Boston paid off exponentially!

In this example, I learned what I needed from the tech support team at the training, not the instructors. Using this new knowledge, I was able to be more successful than if I had just followed the steps in the manual over and over.

The three most important takeaways here are:

- It is essential to remember that frustration is a natural part of learning. If it frustrates you, you know you're on the right track to learn something brand new and benefit from it.

- Training is the *right place to make mistakes.* You have support there to help you learn the correct information and explain the whys and hows of everything, and it's not a high-risk situation when you make a mistake. Mistakes are part of the learning process, and we learn more from failing than from succeeding.

- You can learn from everyone around you, not just managers and trainers, but from anyone skilled. Take advantage: keep your eyes peeled for new things to learn and for people from which to learn.

5.2 The Culture of Learning Matters

Creating a culture of learning means we give employees room to explore, make mistakes, get frustrated, and learn, without causing too much of an impact on the organization. Even though I was very frustrated in Boston, I did have someone holding my hand each time the computer did not work.

They didn't just fix it for me. They guided me to the solution.

Giving our employees room to experiment gives them room to struggle and grow. Provide support. Create a culture of learning so your team can grow and learn.

Join me on the journey to create a culture of learning because such a culture is not a trend; *it is the future of learning*. Together we can define what that looks like for you, your organization, and the groups with which you work.

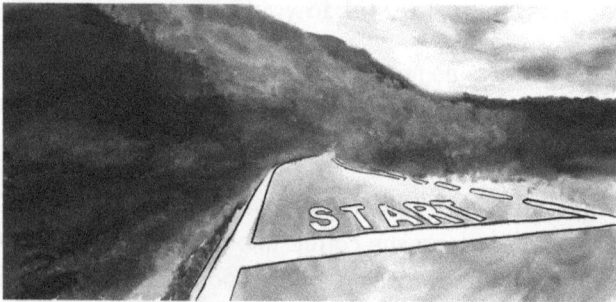

5.3 Learning Profiles

One big hurdle to effective development is determining the learning profile of those with whom you are communicating. When you align with the audience's learning profile, they enjoy the training process. When you don't, they become bored, confused, and even hostile.

If you experience training aligned with your preferred learning profile, you learn more, and you learn faster. Learning doesn't need to be deeply immersive to be valuable but presenting information aligned with a specific learning profile increases the chances your employees will be immersed in the experience.

Creating a culture of learning allows your employees to learn in a manner they enjoy and get the most benefit from. It will be more effective as they engage with content in the method they prefer.

Discovering activities that trigger higher rates of employee learning retention will improve the effectiveness of your learning and development investment.

Since learning is one way to gain a competitive advantage and protect your company's long-term viability, why not maximize its effectiveness by creating learning and development programs that match your employees' learning profiles? As they learn more and you communicate more effectively, trust is built, and collaboration is encouraged. This positions everyone—and the organization—for success.

5.4 What Works?

Companies spend lots of time and money on learning, but very little of it gets implemented in the workplace. Why do we keep building out programs with the least effective type of learning when it is not working? As learning professionals, we should be focused on building learning experiences that work.

For companies to remain viable in the rapidly changing climate, learning must be effective. Formal education in classroom settings will not cut it anymore. We cannot pull employees away from their jobs to engage in training that is ineffective or which doesn't meet the needs of the workplace. We need to build learning into the fabric of what employees do every day. We need to give them guidance and direction to do their jobs in the way we expect.

Complacency will lead to our demise. To protect the jobs of learning and development professionals and ensure the success of the organizations we serve, we owe it to ourselves and them to be proactive and creative in finding ways to determine how to engage employees effectively in meaningful learning. Creating a culture of learning ensures the type of learning delivery method is the most effective for the ones who need to learn.

As you create learning that engages employees and proves itself to be effective, you will become the most coveted department within the organization. Employees will look to you to build their knowledge, skills, and attitudes. Meanwhile, management will look to you to keep the company on track with its organizational goals. Everyone wins when you create a culture of learning where learning is part of everyday activities!

Creating a culture of learning is one of the most vital components for developing ambitious employees. People are motivated and engaged when they are progressing, and learning is the primary driver of progress.

As learners progress along the continuum to mastery, they will be motivated and driven to develop their AQ.

5.5 Examples of Learning Profiles

Let me share three examples demonstrating the value of learning and development and consider different learning profiles. A learning **profile** is different from a learning **style**. We often hear people talk about visual, auditory, and kinesthetic learning as if one person has a preferred way to learn, but these only refer to the different styles or types of learning that exist. Visual aids can enhance the learning experience; if you can only hear what is being taught, then learning is happening in an auditory environment, but the **best** way for **everyone** to learn is hands-on, which is the definition of kinesthetic.

A learning profile is different from a learning style. A learning profile is when we profile people's specific preferences for learning, how they learn best, and where they like to get their information. Let's explore this a bit.

5.6 Listening to Learn

I was hired by a large accounting firm to rebuild an instructor-led learning program and make it available online. I attended a three-day session delivered live by experts who used standard presentation-style delivery. My job was to look for ways to make it more interactive and engaging via online delivery.

After three days of trying to absorb highly technical information, I walked away, literally, with a massive headache. When I got to the airport for my flight home, I was seated next to several attendees in the boarding area. They were chattering on about the last three days. They were excited and invigorated. They thought the previous three days were some of the best of their career.

I was a bit baffled. How could someone appreciate listening to several people drone on for several days about what I thought were technical and boring topics? I took the opportunity to ask them what they felt was so engaging and why they valued the experience. It was quite simple. The presenters were all experts in their field. They brought fresh insight into the topic and gave interesting ways to look at the new methodology accountants would be required to use in their daily practice. They were so excited; they got to sit at the feet of people with vast knowledge and wisdom.

Wow, I thought, *it really is simple for them to learn! Just give them an expert with relevant knowledge and experience and let the expert share.* The learning delivery style matched the audience. As a result, the online course provided access to lots of videos from experts.

Another example is computer and IT specialists. Most of them are avid readers and would rather read a manual than sit in a classroom, although there are times they enjoy learning from an expert. Customer service, sales, and people in general tend to like to learn in a social atmosphere, often with a certain level of competition.

Executives tend to like brief, to-the-point, and results-oriented learning. Time is precious to them, and they do not want filler or fluff. Just teach the information in a brief, concise way and show them how the information will yield results. They'll figure out the rest.

5.7 Learning by Teaching

Several years ago, my son was working for an electrical company. He was new to the profession, as were many of his apprentice coworkers. They were struggling to adhere to the required safety standards. The company hosted safety meetings every Friday where one of the senior-level electricians would present on a safety-related topic. These lectures were still not getting new team members to adhere to safety standards.

My brother was one of the senior-level electricians, and during one of our discussions about safety, I suggested he allow the junior members to conduct the safety meetings. He was shocked at the idea. To alleviate some of his concerns about people who don't follow the rules teaching others to follow required safety standards, I further explained how it would work.

First, each junior team member would be assigned a date to give a short, highly focused presentation on a specific safety topic. Leading up to their presentation date, the senior team members would work with each junior member to prepare their presentation.

The result was the time spent preparing and practicing for their short presentation proved to be an excellent way for the junior members to understand better, retain, and utilize safe practices on the job.

My son explained that while he was delivering his prepared material, people asked him questions, some of which he could answer and others which required him to do research. He was motivated to research because people would **depend** on him to find the answers. He also explained that he learned **from** the discussion because he was **facilitating** the conversation.

*He was fully engaged because he was an **active** participant.*

Moreover, he felt appreciated for his contributions. As a result, the electric company was finally able to move the needle on safety in a positive direction.

5.8 Hands–On Learning

Although everyone learns by doing, some people **require** hands-on practice to master a skill and cannot adequately process the knowledge without it.

Most vocational jobs have "on-the-job" requirements. They provide a small amount of classroom training, but most learning happens on the job. You acquire an apprentice or journeyman status through completing a specified number of hours and documenting job tasks. For example, electricians, plumbers, HVAC, and mechanics all generally start and progress through their careers by accumulating on-the-job hours under direct supervision and meeting specific skill requirements.

Most blue-collar work is learned on the job. For frontline workers in the airline industry, there is typically a small amount of classroom learning, and the rest of the knowledge is gained on the job. Pilots spend hours upon hours in flight simulators, which are a form of on-the-job learning. Flight attendants spend about six weeks in training, most of which is spent practicing service skills, but also, more importantly, practicing evacuating an airplane. Because evacuating an aircraft is not something one does regularly and the outcome is so critical, flight attendants engage in recurrent training every six months to practice those skills, so they are automatic if and when the need arises. Gate agents and ramp personnel start actual work while still under the direction of a mentor to help them complete tasks in the work environment. They may be provided with some scenarios and simulations before engaging on the job, but the vast majority of learning happens through actually doing the job.

Although vocational jobs naturally lend themselves to hands-on learning, ALL jobs are better learned with real-life practice. ALL people learn better with practical experience.

5.9 The Learning Button

I believe the key to finding the right learning profile is to understand your audience by asking questions and observing how they learn best to see what **triggers** their **learning button**.

Those accountants learned faster, and they learned more, when an expert delivered the content they needed to be compliant with new regulations, while the junior electricians learned more quickly by teaching the materials to others. Hands-on learning is the most common method of people learning new **skills**. Different groups of people respond to different types of learning delivery methods.

Give a bunch of introverted data scientists role-playing activities and no matter how well-constructed they are, they may not appreciate the learning experience. They may tolerate it, but not be fully engaged.

I have also learned that when working with computer and IT specialists, many of them prefer to do research on their own, examine the results, and problem-solve based on their findings and experimentation. They might not appreciate sitting in a class where they play games or participate in fun icebreakers.

Sometimes triggering the learning button is enough to get some people through what might otherwise be boring learning. For example, my son went to college right out of high school. He was a good student but was not into the college learning environment. He didn't enjoy sitting in a classroom and talking about things—he wanted to experience things! So, after struggling his first semester in college, he found an emergency medical technician (EMT) course where he absolutely loved attending every session. He is now in Physician's Assistant school and willing to work through the tedious parts because he is motivated. He needed a jumpstart to activate his AQ.

We must find what triggers people's learning button.

5.10 The Importance of Integrated Learning

Coaching—teaching, learning, and leading—can be one of the least costly and most effective methods for developing employees. When you create a culture of learning, effective coaching is an integral part of that culture. Organizations employing a culture of learning realize immediately effective coaching is a primary driver of employee success.

In an article on *Employee Development Statistics*, Monika Hamori, Jie Cao, and Burak Koyuncu of Harvard Business stated, "Dissatisfaction with some employee development efforts appears to fuel many early exits. We asked young managers what their employers do to help them grow in their jobs and what they'd like their employers to do and found some large gaps. Workers reported that companies generally satisfy their needs for on-the-job development and they value these opportunities, which include high-visibility positions and significant increases in responsibility. But they're not getting much in the way of formal development, such as training, mentoring, and coaching—things they also value highly."

As astounding as the results are, L&D professionals fall far short of giving employees what they need and WANT! Employees want their bosses to provide guidance and immediate feedback for their efforts. They want to know how and what to improve so they can perform better.

Several experiences in my career have shown me that workplace coaching is far more powerful than online or classroom learning. Here's an experience where I could have benefited from a more integrated learning approach and effective communication.

A couple of years ago, I started a job and was immediately assigned a mentor. She was currently doing my job, so she was an outstanding asset to my development. She could tell me where to find things, what processes to follow, and how to get myself signed up for a myriad of resources I would need to access while at my new job. I leaned on her heavily for guidance in my position.

That proved to be a tremendous help. What I did NOT receive was instructions on HOW to do my job. Granted, they hired me because I had a specific skill set matching the job description. But the job description was vague and did not specify clear cultural expectations required to do the job. It was a new position, so both the employer and I were feeling our way around this new territory. I thought we were going to be learning together.

I was wrong.

They did have expectations. Those expectations were never clearly articulated to me. They would ask things of me, and when I did not fulfill those expectations, they pulled me from projects with no explanation. When I asked why, they said it was all part of the learning curve. I was not at all clear on what I was supposed to be learning. What could I do differently? I needed real-time feedback from someone who knew the culture and the unwritten rules and expectations.

When I had weekly meetings with my direct supervisor, he always assured me things were fine, but increasingly my job duties were moving down the scale, not up.

What I needed was feedback from a coach, such as a supervisor, who had learned the art of managing expectations and of clearly communicating essential job duties required to fulfill the role. Even if you hire someone with the right skill set, how do you ensure her method of implementing said skill set matches your culture? How do you enable employees to meet YOUR expectations?

The answer lies in communication and learning from an experienced hand in the organization. In a learning culture, communication skills are honed and developed in real-time and not just in a classroom. It comes from the top down: Management is schooled on how to provide effective feedback and to clearly communicate expectations in the moment they are delivering feedback to their employees. Formal training may help fill some of the gaps, but effective management is needed to clearly define job responsibilities and provide effective feedback. A good class can be a great start, but everyone needs real-time, in-the-moment learning while practicing these skills.

CHAPTER 6

DESIGNING AN AMBITIOUS WORKPLACE

An ambitious workplace provides a culture of learning in which team members...well, *learn*. Learning can be conveyed in multiple ways. It must be nurtured, not isolated. In other words, to develop an ambitious workplace, you must make learning part of the overall context of the workplace itself.

The value and effectiveness of your enhanced culture of learning are measured and continually fine-tuned to keep pace with a rapidly changing workforce and competitive pressures. To create ambitious employees, you must foster and develop—as we have said already—a culture of learning. But what does that **look like**?

Before we can deliver a learning culture promoting ambition, we first must understand a few things about learning. We must understand the difference between asynchronous and synchronous learning, we must grasp the various delivery methods for learning, and we must be able to engage our employees. For more on this, please visit my website www.ambitionquotient.com.

6.1 Asynchronous Learning vs. Synchronous Learning

Asynchronous learning is learning conducted by the individual and is independent of others. Through online or mobile learning platforms, reading materials, or a variety of other means, the individual takes time to learn and digest information at his own pace. Examples of asynchronous learning would be someone watching a YouTube video to learn how to repair a broken watch or someone using books and online sources to teach themselves how to code.

Synchronous learning, by contrast, is conducted by instructors in the classroom, at seminars and webinars, and even socially. In other words, it takes place in sync with other people. All people, meanwhile, can mentor, or be mentored, by others, in any of the venues where people interact. This includes in-person, through communication, and on social media. Examples of synchronous learning include people taking a woodworking class together, as well as a group of accounting experts attending a three-day seminar to learn new methods.

Synchronous learning also includes games and simulations allowing us to impart knowledge in the context of achieving some other goal, sometimes shared with others. Simulations can be straightforward, or they can be incredibly immersive, up to and including virtual reality. A competitive aspect may be incorporated to motivate employees to participate. Salespeople typically respond well to competitions, partly because the job itself is somewhat competitive in nature, and they thrive in competitive settings.

People don't alter their behavior instantly or from a single learning opportunity. They must see results—a return on their efforts—and these results must be reinforced in their environments. This is why creating a culture of learning is so vital to creating ambitious employees. Synchronous learning creates intentionality on the part of the organizations, resulting in a culture that ultimately improves behavior and motivation.

6.2 Delivery Methods for Learning

There are so many ways and contexts in which to deliver learning. When I started my career, instructor-led training and job aids were the primary sources of formal learning in the enterprise space. Thus, when you wanted to teach something new to someone, you set up a class. When you supported someone doing something on the job, you had a job aid such as a manual, many of which were used for on-the-job training along with job shadowing. There were a few times when simulations (like flight simulators) were used to practice skills best *not* practiced on the job.

Since then, I've seen many new and exciting ways to deliver training emerge. From online learning to microlearning and massive open online courses (MOOCs) to online simulations, electronic performance support, gaming, webinars, and more. The list is lengthy.

Being something of a maverick myself, I found myself excited to jump on every new emerging trend. Each brought with it exciting new ways to reach people who otherwise might not be getting the learning they needed to stay engaged at work. But what I found was many people wanted to replace the old with the new—just because it was new or would reduce the company's training budget, and not as part of an overall plan for better learning.

Over time, I found that real learning was often hijacked by trends in delivery methods and/or a need to slash budgets. This in turn caused companies to **not** facilitate a culture of learning where employees were excited to learn, acquire more knowledge, and develop an attitude of engagement.

A few years ago, I was contracted to build an onboarding program for new employees of a large energy organization in competition with a rival organization to acquire talent. Both organizations had successful recruiting programs attracting and securing the best and brightest from colleges around the country. But both were losing talent within a short period and had a high turnover rate. Focus group results showed neither company could provide the intellectually challenging environment those students demanded.

Also, the graduates felt like they were not supported with enough resources to do their jobs well. I was brought in to build an onboarding program. This program could not be the traditional three- to five-day in-house program focused on things like where to get a security badge, how to log into a computer, how to access SharePoint, and training for general safety, ethics, and harassment.

These employees wanted to know the people with whom they were working. They wanted to know who had the information they needed to be successful in their jobs. They wanted to know what available resources would enable them not only to perform well today, but also in the future. They wanted to be part of an organization where they felt they were making a difference and having an impact.

They wanted to understand the hows and whys of the business. They expected to be engaged in meaningful projects right from the start. They wanted to feel like they had a say in the future of the company. They didn't just want a job—they wanted *a purpose-driven job.*

This was going to take much more than a week of classroom and online training giving them the "how" to do things, but also the "why" they do things and "what" they could do to improve the products/ services and the workplace.

Estimates show that 70% of enterprise employees worldwide are not engaged at work. In turn, half a trillion dollars are lost each year due to lack of engagement. Twenty-nine percent of millennials (who are rapidly becoming the bulk of employees) are not engaged. This is costing organizations not only in lost revenue, but also in decreased production and high turnover rates.

6.3 A Culture of Learning That Promotes Ambitious Employees

A culture of learning complements formal learning with informal learning that can be incorporated into the employees' daily work routine so new skills, knowledge, and attitudes become habits.

Formal learning (classroom-based learning, seminars, virtual instructor-led learning) is an effective way to introduce new concepts and generate motivation for implementing new programs, but old habits return if formal learning isn't reinforced. Consider a variety of the latest informal learning resources like job aids, white papers, online learning modules, and standard operating procedure manuals along with coaching and mentoring to provide ongoing support and to reinforce formal learning.

Explore the *Art and Science of Learning* to maximize retention and job transfer. Since reinforcement and repetition are the keys to learning that sticks, consider the best ways to implement these techniques into your learning culture. For more on this, please visit my website www.ambitionquotient.com.

Problem-solving, team building, creativity, and communication skills are embedded in many different aspects of an employee's workday. Custom learning paths tailor learning to the person and her current and future job roles.

A culture of learning, in other words, **teaches, rather than preaches, your values**. Gain an understanding of what motivates people to engage with learning. This will lead to higher levels of engagement with the organization.

One of the primary methods of engagement comes when employees are performing well at work and feel like what they are doing is meaningful. People like to contribute and feel valued. Learning is a critical component in facilitating engagement. They perform better when they have the knowledge, skills, and attitudes required to master their job duties. They acquire knowledge, skills, and attitudes through learning.

Also, we can no longer expect those who finish college will, ipso facto, have the knowledge, skills, and attitudes necessary to do their jobs in the upcoming year, or even in the next 12 hours, according to *Industry Tap into News*.

Learning happens in both formal and informal environments. Both serve the employee and employer well when learning experiences are matched with the right delivery mechanism for learning, instead of just going with what is trending or new.

Delivering effective learning which enables people to perform better is more than merely providing information for people to consume in a convenient and simple format. It involves understanding your audience, giving them a reason to engage with the material, and using appropriate delivery methods.

Using focus groups and storytelling exercises, we can explore where high-potential employees get information which helps make them successful. This knowledge in turn identifies the precise knowledge, skills, and attitudes which make them successful. We uncover attributes transferrable to other employees, such as industry knowledge, communication skills, leadership styles, problem-solving, creativity, resilience, and team building. We identify domain and industry knowledge of veteran employees that needs to be transferred to appropriate levels of the company.

A job task analysis survey identifies technical and process skills new employees lack, whether just out of school or already working in your industry. From this, you can create learner profiles based on typical characteristics of various job roles so custom learning can be delivered in a way those job roles learn best.

Research and information from the surveys are used to identify gaps in knowledge, skills, and attitudes of employees, as well as to decide how to fill these gaps in ways that get employees up to speed quickly. You must identify current gaps and build a plan to develop and deliver those materials.

You'll also identify soft skills employers consistently say employees lack when they are hired. Soft skills are also lacking in many new employees who have little work experience. This also allows companies to identify process skills your employees need now and evaluate what resources currently exist to meet those needs. These resources may or may not currently be in the form of formal training materials.

Once a well-defined strategy is in place, you can explore ways to repackage your existing learning resources to accelerate employees' mastery of the knowledge, skills, and attitudes required to keep your company competitive.

My job as a learning and development specialist is to help you develop customized learning ecosystems for each type of employee that are easy to access and use. They are unique to each learner/ employee and enable learners/employees to define their own path to success. When employees are actively engaged in learning and progressing, they are motivated to produce at higher levels.

These solutions are context-sensitive and use responsive technology which customizes the learning experience to each individual and device. This also allows the learner to "learn while doing."

This is how a culture of learning is created, and as you can see, it is directly tied to the qualities you want to—and which you *must*—develop in your personnel. This is the only way your teams can help you accomplish what you cannot accomplish alone.

Delivering learning starts with onboarding, but it does not stop there. It extends to every part of an organization, from customer service to sales and marketing, supply chain and IT, and ultimately, to leadership. Arguably, it must start with leadership to occur in other areas.

6.4 Finding the Missing Quotient

The key to success in the knowledge and digital age is **ambition**. How you choose to capitalize on this asset will chart the course for your organization.

According to the Harvard Business Review, we need to build learning organizations, because learning organizations *promote* ambition. David Garvin identifies several components to developing learning organizations, which he defines as "an organization skilled at creating, acquiring, and transferring knowledge, and at modifying its behavior to reflect new knowledge and insights."

Among those components are:

- Systematic problem-solving, which relies on the scientific method, fact-based management of real data, and statistical tools.

- Experimentation, which tests new knowledge through the scientific method.

- Learning from experience, which means reviewing both successes and failures to capitalize on them.

- Learning from others, which comprises gaining insight from looking outside one's immediate environment to take advantage of new perspectives.

- Transferring knowledge, which means spreading knowledge quickly and efficiently throughout the organization.

Garvin also emphasizes the need to measure learning, quantify the results achieved, and manage the organization's progress based on those outcomes. There are many learning design principles your organization must employ to capture the interest of your employees. This will motivate them to excel in their positions...and this is how we do it.

Salvador Dali famously said, "Intelligence without ambition is like a bird without wings." In other words, an employee who is very skilled will never apply those skills—nor reach their full potential as an individual—without a sense of ambition driving that person forward.

Until now, I have presented concepts promoting ambition in the workplace. To achieve your learning culture's full potential, however, you must be able to implement those concepts. Let's now take a look at what applying ambition means in practical terms.

It would be nice if there were a single solution to a multifaceted approach to learning, but there is no single answer. However, I can give you examples, and you may have to use some of your creative juices to see how this might apply to your specific organization and its culture.

Every industry is different, and every organization is different. Various topics lend themselves to different delivery methods. Keep this in mind as we delve a little deeper into the practical nuts and bolts of the ambitious workplace.

Everyone has to onboard employees. This is a make-or-break time for many employees and employers. According to TLNT, *one-third* of new hires quit their jobs after about six months. During the early stages of your employees' careers, it's critical to outline milestones for your new hires to accomplish. Without these goals in place to help cultivate new employees actively and attentively, it's easy for them to become under-challenged or overwhelmed. In either case, this creates an unnecessarily heavy burden on your recruiters and your employees.

TLNT outlines the following statistics:

- Referred employees have a 45 percent retention rate after two years.

- Seventy-eight percent of business leaders rank employee retention as important or urgent.

- Thirty-three percent of employees knew whether or not they would stay with their companies long-term after their first week.

- Thirty-five percent of employees will start looking for a job if they don't receive a pay raise in the next 12 months.

- Thirty-three percent of leaders at companies with more than 100 employees are currently looking for jobs.

- Thirty-two percent of employers say they expect employees to "job-hop."

How do you retain the fresh new talent and enable them to maintain their enthusiasm and become ambitious employees? The primary motivator for hiring and maintaining ambitious ability is to *give them meaningful work.*

Even when a new team member is highly qualified, beginning a new role without a clear and active direction can drain motivation and decrease productivity. To instill in the newcomers your values, ethics, and processes, they need to be actively engaged. A week-long "training" may not be enough.

6.5 Action Learning

Have you ever heard of Action: Learning? The name implies learning while in action, and this method is essentially learning by doing. Here's a preview of the impact of action learning at work.

6.5.1 Scenario 1: Onboarding without Action Learning

Before considering a scenario that involves action learning, let's look at how onboarding has often been approached. Let's see how Atticus gets acclimated to his new role. This scenario may feel familiar.

Atticus has been hired by a tech company to write contracts for field sales representatives. He has the academic requirements, skills, and experience to fit right into this role, and he's ready to get started.

Day 1: Atticus gets his laptop, badge, and login info, and he starts with some required reading. He meets the team and the people he will eventually go to for legal redlines, product information, shipping questions, privacy concerns, and pricing approvals.

In the following days, Atticus tours the facility, learning about the culture and the products the company sells. He takes mandatory training sessions and learns terms and practices to help him as he writes contracts. There's much information, and he tries to absorb as all he can.

His manager mentions the training sessions aren't exactly up to date with the current processes, as it's an ever-changing landscape out there. Plus, it's hard for any business to continuously capture the knowledge and workflow descriptions needed for these initial training sessions. However, this is how everyone starts. The real learning will come soon.

At the end of his first week, Atticus is still in training meetings, going through faux contract scenarios. He's feeling ready to write agreements, but he's wondering if the content is relevant or up to date. He cannot remember all the appropriate use of language and terminology and is continually flipping through all the notes he took. He's losing interest and motivation because this is feeling like "busy work."

Unfortunately, this onboarding process is all too common.

6.5.2 Scenario 2: Onboarding with Action Learning

For this scenario, let's see how Action Learning can be applied to change the onboarding process.

Atticus has been hired by a tech company to write contracts for field sales reps. He has the academic requirements, skills, and experience to fit right into this role, and he's ready to get started.

Day 1: Atticus gets his laptop, badge, and login info. He meets the team and gets assigned a few experts to shadow for his first week. He has several lunch dates with key stakeholders affecting his job role.

His first agreement is written on Day 1. This isn't a training exercise— this translates to critical work the company needs to accomplish. A mentor shows Atticus where they keep the agreement templates and lets him go through writing his first agreement. The mentor stays with him to help him, answer questions, and check his work, then has him email the deal to the field sales rep who is closing this deal.

His agreements become more and more nuanced. On one agreement, he meets with the legal team to seek approval and edits to some redlines an account has sent over on some purchase quotes. He's learning the business and legal practices of the company as he gets this agreement turned around and back out to the field.

Atticus continues to have subject matter experts nearby, and while he still obtains review and approval for agreements before sending them out, he's feeling motivated. He's written dozens of agreements. His work is immediately valuable to the company and him.

By the end of the week, Atticus has ideas for improving this onboarding process. His feedback and beliefs contribute to the onboarding of the next new employee for his team.

While there's much more to the full process of action learning, the juxtaposition of these onboarding scenarios helps illustrate the importance of learning leading not just to knowledge, but to action.

6.6 Are All the Elements in Place?

You've probably heard it said, "Employees don't quit their jobs; they quit their bosses."

Robert Montenegro cited this when telling the story of Alison McMahon, an HR specialist and CEO of the company TwoFold: "Nine times out of 10, when an employee says they're leaving for more money, it's simply not true," Montenegro writes. "It's just too uncomfortable to tell the truth."

People are willing to put up with the *negatives* of their jobs as long as they enjoy who they're working for, and as long as their work is meaningful. But without hard skills and soft skills, the ambitious employee can't realize his full potential.

6.7 Hard Skills: Hands–On, Practical, and Experiential

In the vocational/trades realm, hands-on training is a must. Not only do the jobs themselves lend themselves to practical experience, the new hires usually learn best by doing rather than reading or analyzing information. The industry already requires a certain number of hands-on hours to achieve apprentice or journeyman status, but before that, they typically have to complete a certain amount of classroom hours.

What if we modified those classroom hours to a minimum of reading and completing job-related tasks, using job aids and videos, with supervision? Computer-based simulation programs allow learners to practice tasks over and over in a fun environment. Many are realistic and provide a variety of scenarios to help prepare the learner for real-life work tasks.

Once on the job, those same job aids and videos can be made available via a tablet to support them when supervisors are not available to remind them how to do tasks. This tablet can become the go-to resource, housing manuals related to various pieces of equipment and their maintenance and operation as well as the skills library. You can also include any organization-specific policies and procedures and vendor information useful when completing projects.

On-the-job checklists are already widely used and help learners see the skills they have already acquired. Using a checklist shows the employees where they are in terms of mastering skills, and also helps them stay on the path to continuous improvement.

A form similar to this one can be utilized. If using an online platform that supports customized learning paths, resources to help them move through the process to mastery can be recommended based on the learner profile and their progress throughout the process. To add an element of fun, use gaming to incentivize their use of resources. Rewards like paid time off, movie passes, restaurant gift cards, and more can work well with this audience.

Keep in mind: this is a high-level, simplified approach to learning that needs to be modified and fleshed out in more detail for your organization and its specific requirements.

Manufacturing, airline, and transportation industries would also benefit from this approach to providing continuous learning opportunities for their employees who are engaged in blue-collar jobs. Employees whose posts require a significant amount of manual labor need ample hands-on practice, easily accessible resources, and many fun ways to practice the skills they need until they reach mastery and can move on to another skill or level.

As these learners move through the continuum to mastery, they will be motivated and driven to develop their AQ.

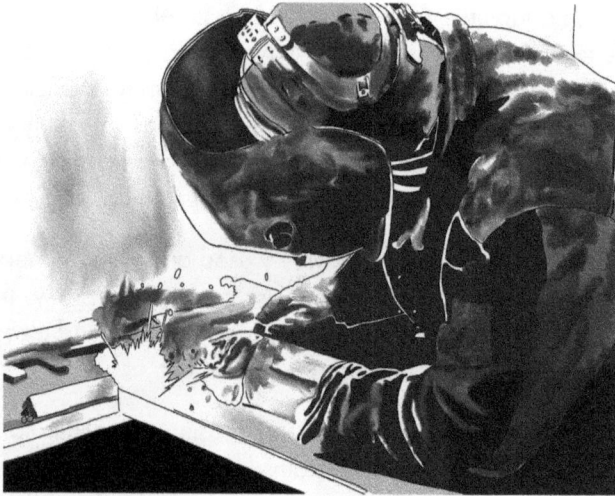

6.8 Soft Skills – Making Effective Decisions

Making effective decisions requires critical thinking skills and analytical reasoning. This is not natural to most people and is typically best taught in the context of the environment in which it is being used. Action Learning or project-based learning can facilitate this type of skill development.

When you need to ensure effective decisions are being made continuously with little to no room for error, the following approach may help.

A healthcare company was losing a significant amount of money because many of the patients in its rehabilitation program were being re-admitted to the hospital for the same issues for which they were initially treated. Their insurance was not covering the cost of readmission, so they were losing millions of dollars each year in readmissions.

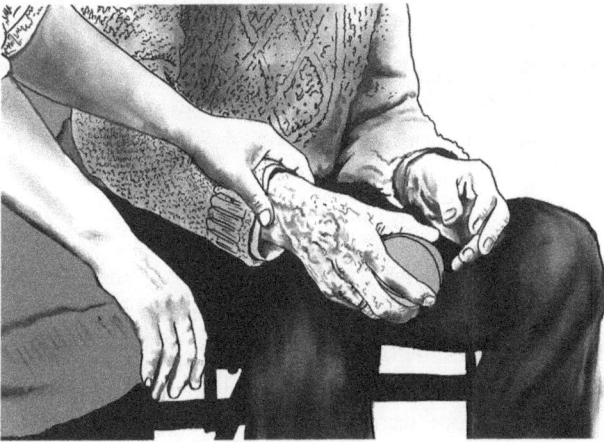

This was in part because the team assigned to make the decision to release the patient was not making effective decisions regarding the transition from the rehabilitation center to home. There were many factors to consider and competing interests from the various doctors, nurses, social workers, and family members. Thus, a scenario-based learning approach was developed to teach team members how to make better decisions.

In this learning, short online modules were developed to introduce the basic guidelines regarding what is termed "transitions in care." From there, videos of team meetings were created with all members of the team sharing their competing interests. In the end, the learners were given a poll question asking them what decision they would make regarding a particular patient and why.

Once they shared their vote and their supporting rationale, they could then see how others in the course voted and their justifications, which spurred online discussions about why each felt their point of view was valid.

Several different patient scenarios were initially developed for all team members to complete. Over time, they would continue to receive new videos sent to them via email with the poll question and discussion board opportunity. They also had easy access through their email to resources to help make decisions. They could comment on these resources, recommend updates, rate the resources, and share them with others. Contributions from subject matter experts to the resource center carried the most weight.

They would also receive, via email, some simple games to help them better understand the policies and procedures and to introduce updates. The wiki became the go-to place for all things related to "transitions-in-care," and it easily linked to the video library and discussion board, where learners could go through the short videos and participate in the poll and discussion boards if they had not yet done so.

Several short videos of successful transitions-in-care would be provided to them periodically to help motivate them to make better decisions because they saw the real-life outcome of their choices. They also earned Continuing Education Units (CEUs) for time spent engaging in this activity.

6.9 Project-Based Learning in Action

Project-based learning is another great way to teach soft skills while also teaching practical industry-related skills. The example of creating a positioning statement listed here is an example of how this could be implemented in the workplace.

Creating a positioning statement to market your organization can be a daunting task, and it requires a significant amount of teamwork and collaboration. This type of activity lends itself well to a project-based learning approach. What better way to learn how to create a positioning statement than to work with your team to create one? Not only do you all learn together, but in the end, you also have a positioning statement for your organization to use when developing marketing strategies and collateral.

A positioning statement is critical for successfully marketing your organization. It is also beneficial for sharing your organization's vision with the team. This is a vital component of setting up your organization for success.

A positioning statement is an articulated expression of how a product, service, or brand is filling a need and how the product, service, or brand stands out from those of competitors.

The four essential elements of a positioning statement are:

1. Description of the target audience

2. A frame of reference or category in which the product, service, or brand competes

3. What makes your product, service, or brand unique (your unique selling proposition)

4. A reason to believe in the product, brand, or service—the best proof you have the company will deliver on its promises

Two example templates of a positioning statement:

• "For (target audience), (brand name) is the (frame of reference) that delivers (benefit/point of difference) because only (brand name) is the (reason to believe)."

- "For (target customer) who (statement of the need or opportunity), the (product name) is a (product category) that (statement of key benefit—that is, compelling reason to buy). Unlike (primary competitive alternative), our product (statement of primary differentiation)."

Throughout the course on positioning, learners are allowed to communicate with others on the team to hone their team-building skills and exercise creativity in applying the principles taught. Throughout the course, resources are available to help the team members when they encounter challenges in this area. They also have access to mentors and coaches who can support them and expand on any resources and concepts.

For example, we teach learners to analyze what their "reptilian brain" is looking for by making sure their positioning statements are unique during the positioning process. Testing for uniqueness is one of the steps in the process we teach: that uniqueness is vital to the part of the brain, the "reptilian brain," actually making decisions.

We help learners to create messages that matter, (www.messagesthatmatter.com) developing the administrative skills which will set them up for success. Positioning and message strategy, overall, are what help set your company or product apart from the competition. Positioning, in other words, is a mental space in your audience's mind. You want to occupy this space with a compelling, meaningful idea. This allows the "reptilian brain" of the customer to make a purchase decision about your product while also helping your customer find the choice meaningful and fulfilling.

CHAPTER 7

CONCLUSION: A GLIMPSE INTO THE FUTURE

Given everything we've learned to this point, the only question remaining is how you will choose to foster an ambitious workplace. You won't do this through technology alone, although technology and other tools can certainly help to accomplish it. Instead, you'll do it as part of fostering a learning environment. Remember, learning is a journey, not a destination. As information and technology rapidly evolve, the need for rapidly changing learning becomes essential.

We inspire ambitious employees by providing them with a customized learning journey. This targets their specific issues and provides them with problems to solve, challenges to overcome, and resources to help them succeed. These resources are presented at the time of need, in context, to maximize retention and transfer from the learning experience to real life.

In other words, the learning is presented to create the type of employees employers want, but they aren't finding in abundance.

This approach presents problems and challenges unique to the participant and his/her detailed learner profile, while recommending resources that enable learning. Resources can include prescribed learning on specific topics or tasks, documents, checklists, peers, mentors, simulations, or friendly competitions, to name a few.

In addition to the essential **knowledge, skills, and attitudes** required for job-specific responsibilities, you must work to develop the vital components necessary for success in any endeavor. As you may recall, these are:

- Creativity
- Problem-Solving
- Teamwork
- Communication
- Resilience

The goal is to provide resources fostering ALL types of learning. Indeed, there are times when formal, prescribed training is helpful and even essential. Remember though: people **learn** by doing, not by just engaging in training. Resources alone are not the solution. We must seek, in creating ambitious employees, to mimic the real world. The answer is based on the learning pedagogy which says people LEARN when presented with challenges and problems to solve, and then utilize the resources available to them to make choices, experiment, and come to solutions on their own.

Creating ambitious employees will prove to be the most valuable initiative your organization undertakes in the next few years. As you work toward giving your employees the knowledge, skills, and attitudes they need, and giving your organization a competitive edge, your team will succeed. Without an ambitious culture, however, your organization will struggle to stay viable in this highly competitive global economy.

This is how we will move forward.

This is how you will create ambitious employees.

This is how we will all succeed.

My company, Read, Write, & Learn Technology, LLC (RWL Tech, LLC), helps employers all over the world look for and cultivate ambition in their employees.

How do your employees rate on the Ambition Quotient scale?

Two minutes of your time will yield valuable insight into some of your organization's most perplexing problems. More importantly, it will help simplify them. Take the FREE quiz now to see how your employees measure up on the scale at www.ambitionquotient.com.

As a bonus, I am offering readers a COMPLIMENTARY "Ambitious Employees Intelligence Quotient Risk Assessment." This is a 60-minute free session to see where your company is now and how you can best create a culture of learning within your company starting immediately.

To qualify for the Ambitious Employees Intelligence Quotient Risk Assessment session:

- Your organization must have more than 50 employees, and

- You must be the person responsible for making decisions about the profitability of your organization and/or the head of HR/ training for your organization.

Reach out to me today at cheryl@smartlearningforbusinesssuccess. com to schedule your FREE 60-minute AIQ Risk Assessment session!

www.smartlearningforbusinesssuccess.com
www.ambitionquotient.com
www.readwritetechnology.com

AUTHOR BIO

Cheryl Johnson is a performance solution specialist with more than 20 years of experience in coaching, learning, development, and workplace training performance. With her pioneering attitude, she has made substantial contributions in the area of learning with an emphasis on behavioral change. Cheryl has been recognized as a leader in the architecture and design of interactive multimedia learning systems and strategies. She was also published by well-known educational psychologist Michael Allen in his 2012 e-Learning Annual. She has dedicated her life to developing learning solutions that drive performance at work and in one's personal life.

In the late 1990s, Cheryl embarked on a journey to create a distance learning program for people using voice recognition technology because it was not cost-effective to train individuals one at a time in remote areas. The technical aspect of the program was primarily developed by a friend and peer and eventually patented. This program is still widely used today in various forms by voice recognition software companies to teach people to use the technology effectively. In the early 2000s, online learning became a much more widely used means of delivering education, and it turned out Cheryl and her friend had been trendsetters.

Cheryl implemented one of the first learning management systems (LMS) in 2005. This LMS has undergone rapid change over the years and is still a critical piece of most organizations' learning programs. She continues to work with a multitude of vendors to implement their technology.

She went back to school in 2008 to learn more about the world of gaming to ensure her knowledge of how to build effective learning using games was up to par before the rush to incorporate gaming into the corporate learning space was introduced.

From 2010-2015, Cheryl spent time fine-tuning the skills she developed over the years and experimenting with various implementations in her environment and at different workplace locations to iron out the wrinkles. She has been actively involved in writing about the future of learning and delivering workshops to prepare interested instructional designers for the coming tsunami of change in the learning world.